"As a successful entrepreneur, I understand the critical role of agility in any thriving organization. Dr. Unhelkar's book affirms and elevates this understanding by intertwining psychological sophistication as a cornerstone of successful agile implementation. This book expertly simplifies complex psychological concepts, making them accessible and actionable within any agile framework. It's a must-add to my collection and a pivotal resource for leaders who aspire to weave agility into the fabric of their organizational culture. Dr. Unhelkar's insightful approach ensures that adopting Agile transcends traditional practices, transforming it into a holistic and transformative organizational ethos."

Andrew Lyman, *Founder, All Point Retail, Florida, USA*

"In light of agility's profound significance, researchers and thinkers must delve into the subject from various perspectives. Bhuvan Unhelkar has admirably accomplished this feat in his book – *The Psychology of Agile*. Including a mind map and psychological frameworks lends breadth to the discussions while exploring Maslow's needs hierarchy and Transaction Analysis provides the necessary depth. This book catalyzes further investigations into the realm of agile."

Anurag Agarwal, *PhD, Professor, Florida Gulf Coast University, USA*

"Dr. Unhelkar offers a fresh perspective on Agile practices, for the first time tying together Agile with psychology, sociology, and organizational theory to develop a new approach to solving industry's most complex problems. *The Psychology of Agile* is fundamental reading for any high-performing leader and a game-changer for innovative organizations. Well done, Dr. Unhelkar."

Andrew Seely, *University of Maryland Global Campus,*
Computer Society Board of Governors Member 2024–2025,
Florida West Coast Section Computer Society Chapter Chair, USA

"As an Investor, Strategic Advisor and Board Member specializing in Digital Transformations, I understand the significance of agile approaches in this field. Recently, I gave a guest lecture to Dr. Unhelkar's graduate class on Agile project management at the Muma College of Business, University of South Florida. I believe that this book will play a crucial role in the success of future Agile leaders, including the ones in the class, who will soon undertake Digital Transformations. The chapters on Agile leadership, organizational structures, and transformations make this book an invaluable resource for all current and future leaders."

Arun Saha, *Managing Partner, 3RP Capital Partners, USA*

"*The Psychology of Agile* offers an insightful examination of the psychological foundations of Agile methodologies, making this book essential reading for both leaders and practitioners of these methods. Connecting theory with practice impeccably, this book offers invaluable insight for anyone attempting to transform organizational culture with Agile – serving as both a comprehensive guidebook and a manual for mastering both this art form and science simultaneously."

Jean Kabongo, *PhD, Associate Dean for Academic Affairs, Accreditation, and Compliance, Muma College of Business, University of South Florida, USA*

"During my part-time MBA program at the University of South Florida, I took a course on Agile project management taught by Professor Unhelkar. It was a great learning experience, and ever since then, I have been applying the principles of agility to my work. I firmly believe that the balanced approach to agility with CAMS is highly practical and effective in complex development and deployment situations. This book further enhances the practicality of agility by exploring the psychological and sociological concepts essential for an agile leader in the digital age."

Joshua Baker, *MBA, Founding Partner, ECO*

"The ability to respond and adapt to circumstances and situations as individuals, small groups, or larger organizations is part of our resilience and success. Such agility, whether in community sports, business, government, or in response to natural disasters and global events, comes from an inherent set of values and a way of thinking and operating within an overall outcomes and behaviors approach. It is refreshing to see a book about agile practices going beyond the standard agile texts and accommodating the diversity of frameworks needed across businesses of all sizes. Working across the business areas using a risk-based approach makes this book of value to the business. Furthermore, the book recognizes the importance of the intrinsic and innate aspects required for sustainable outcomes while supporting the application to practical and diverse business circumstances. From enhancing the prerequisites like project and management and change management to support transformation, this book can also be applied to risk-based areas like finance, audit, regulatory and compliance, and areas like HR."

Keith Sherringham, *Independent Business Consultant and Executive Advisor on Business and Technology Transformation and AI Implementation, Sydney, Australia*

"Professor Unhelkar is a lateral thinker and has demonstrated exceptional skills in this book. This book entails a vivid and comprehensive way of explaining the concept of Agility beyond the four declarations of the Manifesto and applying it to various projects and organizations. With the discussions on psychological frameworks and their application in the agile workplace, this book has a notable social impact. It is a valuable addition to Professor Unhelkar's previous publications in the field of agile, serving as an excellent resource for both practical and research purposes."

Prof Prasun Chakrabarti, *PhD (Engg), Dean, School of Engineering, Director – Research and Publications, Dean, International Affairs and Department of Computer Science and Engineering, Sir Padampat Singhania University, Udaipur, Rajasthan, India*

"As a psychology practitioner, I recognize mindset's vital role in an individual's success. This book delves into the importance of integrating psychology to cultivate a thriving mindset within the fast-paced work environment of modern businesses. The book's unique approach includes easy-to-understand discussions on Transactional Analysis and games, the left and right brain functions, slow and fast thinking, and mapping Maslow's hierarchy of needs to agile transitions. These discussions will positively impact the way we work. Absolutely worth reading!"

Radha Bhatia, *PhD, Clinical Psychologist, New Jersey, USA*

"I have known Bhuvan for over ten years and actually wrote the preface for one of his books on agile, *The Art of Agile Practice*. Bhuvan has written numerous books on business analysis, software development, and emerging technologies. Each one is a master class in the topic, including this one on the psychology of agile. I have always believed that psychology plays an important and often overlooked role in the success of agile software development and its application to the world in general. Bhuvan is right on point with this enlightening and enjoyable exploration of the mindset of agile."

Steve Blais, *Solutions Architect, Systems Consultant, Trainer, and author of* Business Analysis: Best Practices for Success *(John Wiley), http://Essenceoftheba.com*

"The modern world of technology is significantly dependent on AI and machine learning. As the industry evolves, there is an increasing demand for flexibility in methods and the overall work environment. The digital business sector must transform to agility by utilizing data-driven technologies to meet these demands. The digital world's business processes and organizational structures are poised for a seismic change. This publication provides valuable guidance on the required shift in mindset to bring about this change, making it a crucial resource for every professional and for every library worldwide."

Professor Francis Yi-Chen Lan, *PhD, DEcon (Honoris Causa), PhD (UWS), BCom (Hons), President, Fu Jen Catholic University, Taiwan (ROC)*

"With the rapid pace of evolving technology, there is renewed emphasis on psychology and human behavior in every industry, especially in an agile environment. As a workforce optimization professional, I expect that Dr. Unhelkar's work will transform the way we practice agile, as it beautifully highlights the power of incorporating soft factors. This book is a must-have for practitioners!"

Carolynn Lengyel, *MBA, CSSBB*

"Dr. Unhelkar and I collaborated on a book during the COVID-19 pandemic called *Artificial Intelligence for Business Optimization*. Like our previous work, where we emphasized the integration of Natural Intelligence with AI, this book takes a unique human-centric approach. This book highlights the crucial role of people in any initiative's success or failure. The discussions on soft factors in this book emphasize the significance of people in the workplace, particularly in the digital age, where perceptions spread rapidly and opinions change instantly. Dr. Unhelkar effectively combines strong theoretical principles with the practical aspects of agile psychology."

Tad Gonsalves, *PhD, Professor, Department of Information & Communication Sciences, Faculty of Science & Technology, Sophia University, Tokyo, Japan*

"Agility is a crucial aspect of work and play in South Africa, just as it is everywhere else. This book does an excellent job of helping people tap into and develop their inner agility. Psychology and sociology play a vital role in the success of any human endeavor, and adopting an agile way of working is no exception. In today's world of data-driven decision-making, AI-powered technology, and constant cybersecurity threats, agility is more critical than ever for businesses to stay ahead. This book contributes significantly by demonstrating how agility is a fundamental human concept that can be applied to team dynamics, business decisions, and society. Congratulations to Dr. Unhelkar for creating such a seminal work."

Visvanathan Naicker, *PhD, Professor, Information Communication & Technology, Faculty of Business and Management Sciences, Cape Peninsula University of Technology, South Africa*

"The field of psychology is closely intertwined with our daily work and personal lives. As such, it is inevitable that we explore psychological concepts and their applications in work environments. This book, which you currently hold in your hands, is a noteworthy example of such exploration. It is authored by Dr. Unhelkar, a past participant in one of my psychology-related courses and a friend. I have full confidence that his work in this book will have a creative and positive impact on the business and project management world."

Dr. Bhupendra Palan, *MD, DClinHypno, USA;*
Founder & Director of Samatvam Institute of Mind-Body Healing & Healthy Living; Founder & President of Academy of Hypnosis, India

Psychology of Agile

Agile is a mindset and a culture that has evolved beyond software development to encompass all forms of project management, business organizations, defense, and society. In today's fast-paced and ever-changing world, adopting an Agile approach is essential for organizations to thrive and maintain competitiveness. This book aims to extend the concept of Agility beyond the four declarations of the Manifesto and apply it to various projects, organizations, and even society. The book delves into the intricacies of Agile and highlights its significance in modern workplaces. It emphasizes that Agile is more than just a set of tools and techniques; it is a way of thinking and a culture that requires a deep understanding of psychology and sociology.

Key topics discussed:

- Agility as a leadership characteristic and the meta-mind of Agile
- Agile mind-map beyond the manifesto and methods
- Psychological frameworks (Maslow, TA, MBTI, Left-Right, Slow-Fast) relevant to Agile work and psychosocial games at work
- Psychological development and Composite Agile Method and Strategy (CAMS)
- Agile organizational structures and behaviors
- Agile Transformations in the Digital Age

This book is valuable for Agile coaches, mentors, and Scrum Masters looking for more comprehensive answers than what an Agile framework can provide. It is also helpful for business leaders, stakeholders, and product owners who need to deal with ambiguous or unclear issues, as well as project managers and team leaders who already have experience in Agile but feel like something is missing. Additionally, HR professionals and trainers involved in Agile transformation can benefit from this book.

Psychology of Agile

Exploring the Human Element at Work

Bhuvan Unhelkar

CRC Press is an imprint of the
Taylor & Francis Group, an **informa** business

Designed cover image: © Shutterstock

First edition published 2025
by CRC Press
2385 NW Executive Center Drive, Suite 320, Boca Raton FL 33431

and by CRC Press
4 Park Square, Milton Park, Abingdon, Oxon, OX14 4RN

CRC Press is an imprint of Taylor & Francis Group, LLC

© 2025 Bhuvan Unhelkar

Reasonable efforts have been made to publish reliable data and information, but the author and publisher cannot assume responsibility for the validity of all materials or the consequences of their use. The authors and publishers have attempted to trace the copyright holders of all material reproduced in this publication and apologize to copyright holders if permission to publish in this form has not been obtained. If any copyright material has not been acknowledged please write and let us know so we may rectify in any future reprint.

Except as permitted under U.S. Copyright Law, no part of this book may be reprinted, reproduced, transmitted, or utilized in any form by any electronic, mechanical, or other means, now known or hereafter invented, including photocopying, microfilming, and recording, or in any information storage or retrieval system, without written permission from the publishers.

For permission to photocopy or use material electronically from this work, access www.copyright.com or contact the Copyright Clearance Center, Inc. (CCC), 222 Rosewood Drive, Danvers, MA 01923, 978-750-8400. For works that are not available on CCC please contact mpkbookspermissions@tandf.co.uk

Trademark notice: Product or corporate names may be trademarks or registered trademarks and are used only for identification and explanation without intent to infringe.

Library of Congress Cataloging-in-Publication Data
Names: Unhelkar, Bhuvan, author.
Title: Psychology of agile : exploring the human element at work / Bhuvan Unhelkar.
Description: First edition. | Boca Raton, FL : CRC Press, 2025. |
Includes bibliographical references and index.
Identifiers: LCCN 2024023583 (print) | LCCN 2024023584 (ebook) |
ISBN 9781032062839 (hardback) | ISBN 9781032062846 (paperback) |
ISBN 9781003201540 (ebook)
Subjects: LCSH: Organizational change. | organizational behavior.
Classification: LCC HD58.8 .U54 2025 (print) | LCC HD58.8 (ebook) |
DDC 658.4/06–dc23/eng/20240523
LC record available at https://lccn.loc.gov/2024023583
LC ebook record available at https://lccn.loc.gov/2024023584

ISBN: 9781032062839 (hbk)
ISBN: 9781032062846 (pbk)
ISBN: 9781003201540 (ebk)

DOI: 10.1201/9781003201540

Typeset in Sabon
by Newgen Publishing UK

Priyanka "Pinka"
Carolynn
Tejal "Pari"

Contents

Foreword

We are both practicing Agile professionals with different industrial verticals: Financial for Josh and HR Contact Centers for Carolynn. We both had the privilege of learning Agile from Dr. Unhelkar, so we were honored and delighted when he approached us to write the foreword for the book. Dr. Unhelkar is a professor, practitioner, and a deep thinker of Agile. As students and close friends, we consistently see how Agile has become part of his DNA. His course materials, learning objectives, and expectations are Agile, adjusting to his diverse students' learning styles and preferences. His communication and approach to building relationships are agile based on his worldwide professional experiences. He has embraced the Agile manifesto beyond business and genuinely practices what he preaches. We are witness to his many incredible accomplishments, including making detailed plans, seeing them to fruition, taking the path less traveled, welcoming change, and enjoying the journey.

Dr. Unhelkar wants it to be known that this is a practitioner's book, and we could not agree more. The book in your hand, "The Psychology of Agile," seeps in practical thoughts, advice, and insights from the author's experiences. As its subtitle says, this book is invaluable for enhancing our experiences at work. We have been privy to these thought processes, have discussed the topics at length, and have successfully implemented these Agile concepts in our respective work environments. In this book, you will discover the tremendous importance of the psychological and sociological factors imperative for agile success. You will also find the concepts explained logically and made easy to apply without needing a background in psychology. As the world continues to evolve and become increasingly uncertain, the ability to predict outcomes with precision is more challenging than ever before. This is particularly true in the business landscape, where automation and artificial intelligence have increased the criticality of agility and flexibility. In today's digital world, pivoting quickly to a changing market is essential for survival. This is where Agile comes into play. While Agile has always been a part of our psychology, it was not until recently that it was given a name. What we may not have realized is that the world has always been Agile. Our psychological instinct to mitigate loss has made us agile in our approach to problem-solving. However, in practice, the Agile methodology can be challenging to implement. Practitioners tend to pick and choose which parts of Agile methodology and manifesto they connect to personally or which suit their current needs. It is viewed as a tool, and the people on the "Agile team" have titles and roles that convey a level of authority and accountability. The partial acceptance of Agile is where the project execution has widely varying results. Many individuals feel more comfortable with a waterfall-style project than an Agile one because it incorporates an illusory sense of control. Rigid processes and metrics are deemed necessary to ensure employees are held accountable for working correctly because the concept of "trust" is not inherent. This hybrid approach leads to subjectivity in Agile. This book brings forth this subjectivity and presents techniques and insights to anticipate and handle it. While Agile is imperative for the intricacies of managing a rapidly changing world, the need for a well-rounded approach that strikes a balance between formality and agility in the workplace is also very well known. The book refers to the Composite Agile Method and Strategy (CAMS) that emphasizes this balance. Leaders can implement CAMS alongside the easy-to-use concepts of psychology and sociology in their daily work routines. The book provides practical insights into navigating this shift, highlighting the benefits of Agile in today's market and the challenges that come with it. It is a valuable resource, especially for leaders struggling with hybrid waterfall and Agile approaches, because it effectively articulates that the foundation of Agile is the appreciation of the emotional human factor. Innovation requires intrinsic human motivation, which can be stifled when leaders micromanage and continually align rewards and consequences to every action. Employees need to have the psychological safety to fail and learn to ultimately succeed. The Psychology of Agile helps leaders view Agile as not just a method of project management, but a way to lead. This book is an excellent resource for leaders, managers, and individuals looking to embrace the Agile methodology and incorporate its principles into their work. It is a must-read for anyone who wants to stay ahead of the curve in today's rapidly changing business landscape. We have already done that!

Joshua Baker
Senior Wealth Business Analyst at Truist

Carolynn Lengyel, MBA, CSSBB
Executive Director, Workforce Optimization

Preface

We do not live in a physical world that can be organized in neat rows and columns. Instead, it is a metaphysical world with built-in human chaos, human contradictions, and human complexity that do not lend themselves to measures and control. This inherently subjective human nature forms the undercurrent of work environments and invariably supersedes external objectivity. However, such a situation should not deter us from attempting to organize our work environment. Efforts to organize subjectivity lead to the development of a system, a method, and a framework. Agile, as a method or a framework, is an honest attempt to cater to the subjectivity of human nature to produce value. As a result, Agile transcends the description of a method or framework and evolves into a craft and art form. Unlike a straightforward method, Agile must be understood as a culture complete with all its complexities and contradictions. Music and painting are more akin to Agile than bridge-building. Agile, therefore, requires a deep understanding of psychology and sociology.

This book aims to take the concept of Agility beyond the four declarations of the Manifesto and apply it to various projects, organizations, and even society. While initially developed for software, Agile has since expanded to encompass all forms of project management, business organizations, defense, and society. Consider, for example, Bruce Feiler's TED Talk on Agile parenting.[1] Feiler draws inspiration from Agile software programming and recommends adopting flexible family practices that promote open communication, encourage feedback from all members, and foster accountability. His unique and innovative approach to managing the daily pressures of modern family life includes encouraging his children to set their own goals and accept the consequences of not achieving them.

This book delves into the psychosocial intricacies of Agile and highlights its significance in modern workplaces. It emphasizes that Agile is more than just a set of tools and techniques; it is a way of thinking and a culture

1 Ted Talk entitled "Agile Programming – For Your Family." Feiler, B. www.ted.com/speakers/bruce_feiler

that requires an understanding of psychology and sociology. The importance of approaching Agile with a humble mindset (humility) cannot be overemphasized as we deal with the complexity of human behavior that cannot be easily defined. The book takes readers on a journey into the meta-mind of Agile, exploring its fundamental principles and beyond. It offers practical advice on applying psychology and sociology theories in an Agile workplace and examines leadership and facilitation techniques that encourage meta-mind and mindfulness.

The Agile approach prioritizes effective leadership, coaching, and collaboration. In an Agile environment, individual contributions are highly valued, making strong leadership a crucial component of success. Agility fosters and leverages exceptional leadership to drive results, and in an Agile context, a leader serves as a catalyst whose influence is pivotal to achieving positive outcomes.

This book also delves into transitioning to an Agile organization, which involves discussions about trust and collaboration beyond project scenarios, infrastructure, and operations and embedding agility in everyday business practices. At an organizational level, embracing an Agile culture is a strategic decision considering key objectives and reasons for agility. It envisions an organization that upholds work ethics and social norms while incorporating necessary ROI calculations to justify the risks associated with expanding the scope of agility. This book emphasizes that the Agile culture provides maximum value at the organizational level, enabling businesses to respond to change, become Lean, and collaborate across verticals. Adopting Agile requires a careful iterative and evolutionary approach that embraces contradictions and failures while fostering creativity. At the organizational level, Agile is genuinely cross-disciplinary. The book explores psychosocial concepts like Maslow's needs hierarchy, left-/right-brain theory, transactional analysis (TA), and high/low context cultures to accomplish this.

A Composite Agile Method and Strategy (CAMS) is necessary to achieve a holistic approach. This book includes an updated mind-map of Agile and a skills-attitude-experience-influence matrix for successful Agile adoption. You can experience the benefits of a robust Agile strategy across your entire organization with the help of this book. Drawing on my experiences working with client organizations and undertaking research in this space, I aspire for you to "be Agile" rather than just "learn" and "do" Agile. Whether you're a large bank, an insurance organization, or a small travel agency with outsourced development, adopting Agile as an organizational culture is vital. With this book, you'll gain the insights and strategies you need to succeed at this different ball game of Agile implementation.

About the author

Bhuvan Unhelkar (BE, MDBA, MSc, PhD) is a professor at the Muma College of Business, University of South Florida; an adjunct professor at Western Sydney University; and an honorary professor at Amity University, India. He is also an accomplished IT professional and Founding Consultant at *MethodScience*. Unhelkar holds a Certificate-IV in TAA and TAE, Professional Scrum Master – I, SAFe (Scaled Agile Framework for Enterprise) Leader, and is a Certified Business Analysis Professional® (CBAP of the IIBA).

His industry experience includes banking, finance, insurance, government, and telecommunications, where he develops and applies Industry-Specific Process Maps, Business Transformation Approaches, Capability Enhancement, and Quality Strategies.

Unhelkar has authored numerous executive reports, journal articles, and 27 books with internationally reputed publishers including *Artificial Intelligence & Business Optimization* (Taylor and Francis/CRC Press, USA, 2021), *Software Engineering with UML* (Taylor and Francis/CRC Press, USA, 2018), and *Big Data Strategies for Agile Business* (Taylor and Francis/CRC Press, USA, 2017); and several Executive Reports (published by *Cutter* – now *Arthur D. Little*) including *Psychology of Agile (two parts)*, *Agile Business Analysis (two parts)*, *Collaborative Business & Enterprise Agility*, *Avoiding Method Friction*, and *Agile in Practice – A Composite Approach*. He is also passionate about coaching senior executives, training, re-skilling, and mentoring IT and business professionals, forming centers of excellence, and creating assessment frameworks (SFIA-based) to support corporate change initiatives. He has led several BABOK, Agile, CAMS, and SAFe training workshops.

Unhelkar is an engaging presenter who delivers keynotes, training seminars, and workshops that combine real-life examples based on his experience with audience participation and Q&A sessions. These industrial training courses, seminars, and workshops add significant value to the participants and their sponsoring organizations because the training is based on practical experience, a hands-on approach, and accompanied by ROI metrics. Consistently ranked high by participants, the seminars and workshops have been delivered globally to business executives and IT professionals in Australia, the USA, Canada, Norway, the UK, China, India, Sri Lanka, New Zealand, and Singapore. Unhelkar is the winner of the IT Writer Award (2010), Consensus IT Professional Award (2006), and Computerworld Object Developer Award (1995). He also chaired the *Business Analysis Specialism Group* of the Australian Computer Society.

Unhelkar earned his PhD in "object orientation" from the University of Technology, Sydney. His teaching career spans undergraduate and master's levels. He has designed and delivered courses including *Global Information Systems*, *Agile Method Engineering*, *Object Oriented Analysis and Design*, *Business Process Reengineering*, and *New Technology Alignment* in Australia, the USA, China, Malaysia, and India. Online courses designed and delivered include the Australian Computer Society's distance education program, the M.S. University of Baroda (India) Master's program, and numerous courses, including *Agile Project Management* and *Business Analysis* at the University of South Florida, USA.

He supervised seven successful PhD students at Western Sydney University and one at DD University, Nadiad, India. He has published numerous research papers and case studies.

Professional affiliations:

- Fellow of the Australian Computer Society (elected to this prestigious membership grade in 2002 for distinguished contribution to the field of information and communications technology), Australia
- Associate Editor, IT Professional (an IEEE Publication)
- IEEE Senior Member, Tampa Chapter, USA
- Life member of the Computer Society of India (CSI), India
- Life member of Baroda Management Association (BMA), India
- Member of Society for Design and Process Science (SDPS), USA
- Rotarian (Past President) at Sarasota Sunrise Club, USA; Past President of Rotary Club in St. Ives, Sydney (Paul Harris Fellow; AG), Australia
- Discovery volunteer at NSW Parks and Wildlife, Australia
- Previous TiE Mentor, Australia

Unhelkar speaks and writes fluently in four languages: English, Hindi, Marathi, and Gujarati. He loves Indian music, poetry, and literature.

Previous Books by B. Unhelkar, published by CRC Press (Taylor & Francis):

[1] **Unhelkar**, B., and Gonsalves, T., 2021, *Artificial Intelligence for Business Optimization*, Routledge, Taylor & Francis Group, USA

[2] Hazra, T., and **Unhelkar**, B., 2020, *Enterprise Architecture & Digital Business*, CRC Press, UK

[3] Sharma, S., Bhushan, B., and **Unhelkar**, B., 2020, *Security and Trust Issues in Internet of Things: Blockchain to the Rescue*, Edited, CRC Taylor and Francis Group, USA

[4] Tiwary, A., and **Unhelkar**, B., 2018, *Outcome Driven Business Architecture,* CRC Press (Taylor and Francis Group/an Auerbach Book), Boca Raton, FL, USA (Co-Authored)

[5] **Unhelkar**, B., 2018, *Software Engineering with UML,* CRC Press (Taylor and Francis Group/an Auerbach Book), Boca Raton, FL, USA (Authored), Foreword Scott Ambler. ISBN 978-1-138-29743-2

[6] **Unhelkar**, B., 2018, *Big Data Strategies for Agile Business,* CRC Press (Taylor and Francis Group/an Auerbach Book), Boca Raton, FL, USA (Authored), ISBN: 978-1-498-72438-8 (Hardback), Foreword Prof. James Curran, USFSM, Florida, USA

[7] Unhelkar, B., 2011, *Green ICT Strategies & Applications: Using Environmental Intelligence,* CRC Press (Taylor and Francis Group/ an Auerbach Book), Boca Raton, FL, USA, April, 2011 (Authored) ISBN: 9781439837801

[8] **Unhelkar**, B., 2013, *The Art of Agile Practice: A Composite Approach for Projects and Organizations,* CRC Press (Taylor and Francis Group/an Auerbach Book), Boca Raton, FL, USA (Authored), ISBN 9781439851180, Foreword Steve Blais, USA

[9] **Unhelkar**, B., 2009, "Mobile Enterprise Transition and Management," Taylor and Francis (Auerbach Publications), Boca Raton, FL, USA, 393 pages, ISBN: 978-1-4200-7827-5 (Foreword by Ed Yourdon, USA)

[10] **Unhelkar**, B, 1999, *After the Y2K Fireworks: Business and Technology Strategies*, CRC Press, Boca Raton, USA, July 1999, total pages: 421 (Foreword by Richard T. Due, Alberta, Canada)

Acknowledgments

Abbass Ghanbary
Amit Tiwary
Anand Kuppuswami
Andy Lyman
Anurag Agarwal
Arun Saha
Asim Chauhan
Aurilla Aurelie Arntzen
Bhargav Bhatt
Bharti Trivedi
Carolynn Lengyel
Channa Achilingam
Chinmay Chatraborty
Colleen Berish
Daniel A.Thuraiappah
Deepak Thakkar
Ekata Shah
Girish Nair
Haydar Jawad
Javed Matin
Jean Kabongo
Jimmy Singla
Josh Baker
Kashyap Kocharlakota
Kamal Gulati
Keith Sherringham
Mohammed Maharmeh
Motilal Bhatia
Mukesh Prasad
Nitin Hardikar
Nosh Mistry
Pooran Chandra Pandey

Pradeep Chhawcharia
Prasun Chakrabarti
Radha Bhatia
Rajeev Arora
S.D. Pradhan
Sachin Tayade
San Murugesan
Sandeep Ranjan
Siva Shankar Subramanian
Shailesh Chitnis
Steve Blais
Sumit Chakravarty
Sunil Jha
Sunita Lodwig
Tad Gonsalves
Tim Weil
Tushar Hazra
Vipul Kalamkar
Visvanathan Naicker
Vivek Eshwarappa
Walied Askarzai
Warren Adkins
Yi-Chen Lan
Zahid Iqbal

Family:

Thanks to my family for their support and good wishes: Asha, Sonki, Keshav, Chinar, and my awesome neighbors Nancy & George Hogreff and Al & Janalee Heinemann.

This book is dedicated to three extraordinary young ladies with a profound understanding of human psychology that cannot be concealed.

Abbreviations

Term/Acronym	Description and Comments
AI	Artificial Intelligence
BABOK	Business Analysis Body of Knowledgew
BPMN	Business Process Modeling Notations
BPR	Business Process Reengineering
BYOD	Bring Your Own Device
CAMS	Composite Agile Method and Strategy
CASE	Computer Aided Software Engineering
CPM	Critical Path Method
MBTI	Myers–Briggs Test Indicator
ML	Machine Learning
PERT	Project Evaluation and Review Technique
PMBOK	Project Management Body of Knowledge
SAFe	Scaled Agile Framework
SDLC	Software Development Life Cycle
WBS	Work Breakdown Structure

Readers

Here are some categories of readers who may find this book useful (this list is not exhaustive):

a. Agile coaches, mentors, and Scrum Masters who are seeking more answers than what a contemporary Agile framework provides.
b. Business leaders, stakeholders, and product owners who deal with ambiguous or unclear issues.
c. Project managers and team leaders who already have experience in Agile but feel like something is missing.
d. HR professionals and trainers who deal with human elements at work.
e. Solutions developers and team members who work in an Agile environment.

Key takeaways of this book

With the material in this book, you will learn how to enhance your leadership skills in an agile environment. Specially, you will be able to:

1. Understand Agile as a natural human characteristic that is subjective.
2. Discover the benefits of Agile beyond software projects for businesses.
3. Accept that Agile provides maximum value at the organizational level.
4. Gain knowledge of the psychology and sociology behind Agile work culture to enhance its practical use.
5. Learn about the memory mechanisms that impact how we interact and collaborate in an Agile work environment.
6. Understand biases in decision-making and how they affect group dynamics in an Agile workplace.
7. Use transactional analysis as a practical framework for Agile communication.
8. Map Maslow's hierarchy of needs, Myers–Briggs (MBTI), Left-Right brains, and Slow-Fast thinking to Agile work.
9. Understand the significance of balance in Agile through the Composite Agile Method and Strategy (CAMS).
10. Appreciate the intersection between digital transformation and Agile transformation.

Chapter 1

Leadership and agility

A balancing act

CHAPTER SUMMARY

The psychology of Agile is a soft capability crucial for effective leadership in Agile work environments and digital transitions. Agile capabilities grow iteratively through discussions, contemplations, case studies, and experience. Agile leadership capabilities apply to projects, organizations, industries, and society. This chapter sets the tone for exploring the psychology of Agile in practice. The premise for this discussion is that the leadership capability is fuzzy and subjective, and the psychosocial phenomena that influence it are difficult to parameterize. Agile leadership, this chapter argues, is an art form dealing with human behavior, culture, synthesis, and balance. This chapter is, therefore, a bold attempt to bring forth the key, non-quantifiable aspects of the psychology in Agile work environments.

INTRODUCTION

The concept of "Agile" came to prominence because of the innate need of businesses to respond to rapid changes. As Toffler described decades ago, it is not just the change but the increasing rate of change confronting business organizations and society.[1] With breathtaking advances in Artificial Intelligence (AI), Machine Learning (ML), and Big Data; the complexities of 5G and 6G networks; and Cybersecurity challenges, leaders and decision-makers face a rapidly moving target. Agile has emerged as an effective way to develop solutions that can satisfy the needs of this dramatically changing business world. Agile worked well in projects to build solutions as it provided visibility, the iterative release of product slices, and trimmed the cellars of documentation. The agile way of working has become so popular that it is now eagerly welcomed to become part of businesses' operations. Agility has evolved into a work culture that transcends project boundaries

1 Toffler, A., 1970, *Future Shock*, Random House, New York.

DOI: 10.1201/9781003201540-1

and is now an integral part of the fabric of business organizations.[2] The chances of agility percolating in society are also high because of the values it brings to human behavior.

With the increasing popularity of Agile and its widespread use come the challenges of leading, transitioning, and managing such Agile work environments. Business organizations are inherently complex, and the advent of AI, Big Data, xG networks, Cloud, Blockchains, and Cybersecurity only make it more so. The COVID-19 pandemic and other external events further add to the difficulties of developing solutions and operating businesses. Building and deploying solutions for complex projects are daunting in such challenging circumstances. The challenges of leadership are further compounded in an Agile project because traditional project management techniques based on hierarchical team structures and the "carrot and stick" levers are not available. The Agile environment can often lead to confusion and perplexity for team members and leaders. Untangling these challenges requires a deep understanding of the underlying philosophy of Agile and the psychology of human behavior. It is crucial to leverage insights from psychology and sociology to develop effective leadership capabilities. Shedding light on the psychosocial dynamics helps leaders navigate project complexities and agile transformations. This chapter explores the nuanced nature of Agile work environments, poses pertinent questions on existential intelligence, highlights the significance of synthesis, elucidates the technology-methodology-sociology of work, and introduces the Composite Agile Method and Strategy (CAMS)[3] as a balancing act.

Humans at work

DeMarco and Lister,[4] Weinberg,[5] Constantine,[6] and Unhelkar[7] have emphasized the importance of addressing "human issues" at work. Human behavior is highly complex, driven by often hazy and ever-changing context and motivations. The complexity of human needs is difficult to quantify

2 Unhelkar, B., 2013, *The Art of Agile Practice: A Composite Approach for Projects and Organizations*, CRC Press (Taylor and Francis Group/an Auerbach Book), Boca Raton, FL, USA, ISBN 9781439851180.

3 Unhelkar, B., 2013, *The Art of Agile Practice: A Composite Approach for Projects and Organizations*, CRC Press (Taylor and Francis Group/an Auerbach Book), Boca Raton, FL, USA, ISBN 9781439851180.

4 DeMarco, T., and Lister, T., 1987, *Peopleware: Productive Projects and Team*, Dorset House, New York.

5 Weinberg, Gerald M., 1998, *The Psychology of Computer Programming*, Dorset House, New York.

6 Constantine, L., 1995, *Constantine on Peopleware* (Yourdon Press Computing Series), Prentice Hall Ptr, Saddle River, NJ; Constantine, L., Panel on "Soft Issues and Other Hard Problems in Software Development," *OOPSLA'96*, San Jose, CA, USA, October 1996.

7 Unhelkar, B., 2003, *Games IT People Play*, Information Age, Publication of the Australian Computer Society, June/July 2003, pp. 25–29.

and, therefore, is likely to be hidden in a work environment. The popular adage "that which you cannot measure, you cannot control" may be true but is insufficient in developing a good leadership approach in Agile. This is because, more often than not, "that which you cannot measure is precisely what drives and motivates the core human behavior." The immeasurable is invaluable in almost all human endeavors. Talents can often be overlooked, and support can be shortchanged because the leaders may need to grasp non-measurable human motivators fully. Understanding those fuzzy human elements that cannot be measured is vital for agile leadership as these human issues play a significant role in successfully launching solutions, bringing about agile transitions, ensuring compliance, and, above all, changing the mindsets.

Philosophically, Agile provides a fresh perspective on work compared to formal, planned project management approaches such as PMBOK,[8] Six Sigma,[9] and PRINCE2[10] Agile has minimal rules to follow and maximum adaptability and flexibility aimed at providing value. Contemporary project requirements often need to be clarified, especially because they are rapidly changing, and those responsible for specifying them may not have a complete picture of what is required at the start of an initiative. Developing a solution based on those requirements is an exercise of close coordination between those who specify and those who produce that solution. Additional coordination is required with those who configure and deploy them, those who use them, and those who ensure compliance with myriad regulations.

Agile work environments handle the aforementioned challenges in unique ways. For example, agile teams are necessarily cross-functional, bringing together expertise from different disciplines to co-locate and work together. Agile teams work on minimum requirements at a time, only essential designs, and develop a working solution throughout the project. At the end of each iteration, when the release is deployed, the users have something tangible to observe, execute, and iteratively provide feedback that goes into the next development iteration. An iterative and incremental lifecycle is at the heart of an agile work environment. Such iterations and increments, together with the close collaboration between individuals, reduced priority on tools and contracts, and acceptance of change, makes agile what it is today – a highly popular way of work. Agile is akin to creating a pathway in an uncertain world rather than following a well-trodden path. As a result, agility requires leaders to pay close attention to the nuances of those individual behaviors. Personal needs, fears, biases, cultural backgrounds, and the resulting group dynamics come into play in agile. Effective Agile leadership facilitates work that balances individual motivation and organizational goals with sensitivity to human behavior. Agile leaders prioritize their people over tools,

8 *The Project Management Body of Knowledge (PMBOK)* (5th ed.), www.pmi.org.

9 Pyzdek, T., 2014, *The Six Sigma Handbook* (4th ed.), McGraw-Hill Education.

10 Office of Government Commerce, 2017, *Managing Successful Projects with PRINCE2.*

emphasizing collaboration over staying within a set time and budget and accepting change over sticking to a rigid plan. When leaders prioritize people, it helps create great organizations that are efficient and effective because they function with a good understanding of human behavior.

Agile is a way of work

The software development community put together Agile. However, agility as a working trait has transcended project-based work, and it is now a way of working that extends to the entire organization. Agility is not new, as such, because it's deeply ingrained in human nature and centers around flexibility and creativity. The agile approach acknowledges, prioritizes, respects individuals, promotes cross-functional collaboration, embraces change, and encourages iterations. Agility lays the foundation for adaptability and change, which are crucial for individual and organizational survival and growth. Agile has evolved into a culture and value system widely accepted and embraced at all levels of an organization. Businesses adopt Agile as a way of working that yields tangible value. Agile organizations are better equipped to weather major disruptions such as the COVID-19 pandemic than rigid, planned, hierarchical organizations. Agile organizations are also better equipped to utilize and capitalize on the tsunami of Big Data, data analytics, and data-driven decision-making. Leaders consider agility a complementary skill and perceive it as a culture and a way of working.

The Agile Manifesto brought about a change in the mindset of an entire generation of people at work.[11] This manifesto has shifted leaders' focus from rigid and planned approaches to more collaborative, communicative, and trust-based practices. As a result, development projects are no longer obsessed with excessive upfront planning, analysis paralysis, and siloed work products predominantly driven by the Waterfall lifecycle. Agile brought an iterative and incremental approach based on collaboration, resulting in more practical, value-added solutions that align with the business needs. This change to the way work is carried out has far exceeded the manifesto's original vision. Agility is a process and mindset that enables continuous improvement and learning and has become popular in projects and also in business operations.

PSYCHOLOGY OF AGILE

The increasing popularity of agile poses some interesting challenges. To begin with, the values of Agile, which are derived from the Agile Manifesto, are difficult to measure. Another challenge is that Agile's iterative and incremental nature does not support detailed and lengthy planning. The agile work environment is increasingly adopting a collaborative approach that

11 agilemanifesto.org.

requires significant trust among individuals compared to the traditional, planned ways of working. When trust, honesty, simplicity, and courage are introduced as agile values, the psychosocial traits of a workplace become fuzzier and require significantly greater awareness. The significance of the psychology of agile methodology becomes evident in this context.

The realm of psychology delves into the intangible emotions of individuals, which cannot be fully explained or measured. As a result, many workplaces that were based entirely on outputs following the rigors of a method neglected these emotions entirely. Agile psychology, on the other hand, welcomes the emotional aspect of work and is specifically focused on this unquantifiable aspect of organizational environments. The psychosociology of Agile makes a clear demarcation between leadership and management, prioritizing the former. This emphasis on leadership is most helpful in using popular agile frameworks, such as Scrum,[12] that emphasize collaboration and accept fuzziness at work. For instance, a ScrumMaster is not a manager but a coach, facilitator, and leader for a group of self-motivated individuals. This role is often described as that of a servant-leader.[13] The critical yet elusive values of agile revolutionize the work style, emphasizing leadership that transcends the rigid reliance on task-based metrics. Agile leadership places coaching and collaboration above excessive planning and task management. Agile psychology justifies and supports the shift in mindset from focusing on tasks and goals to cultivating a joyful, supportive, and collaborative work environment. Agile leaders seek successful outcomes as a natural byproduct of a fulfilling work environment.

The Agile Manifesto offers a set of principles to organizations that want to adopt Agility without following a rigid framework. To do this, leaders must understand the psychology and sociology of individuals and groups and their role in being agile. One of its main principles is prioritizing individuals and interactions over processes and tools. While processes and tools are important for work, they should not be the main focus. Agility emphasizes communication and collaboration to achieve success. B.F. Skinner's[14] arguments on the insistence of scientific methods to bring about change and that free will is illusory are easily countered by smart and adaptable agile leaders. For successful agile transitions leaders must understand the importance of allowing individuals to exercise their free will within their professional work. Agile methodologies encourage individuals to express their creativity while taking responsibility for their actions. Unlike traditional initiatives prioritizing excessive planning and productivity metrics, agile methodologies recognize the fundamental human need for flexibility and adaptability. This is a key reason for agile's growing popularity in the digital age. It offers a new and adaptable paradigm for organizing teams and

12 www.scrum.org.

13 *The Scrum Guide*, www.Scrum.org.

14 Skinner, B. F., 2002, *Beyond Freedom and Dignity*, Hackett Publishing, Indiana, USA.

businesses.[15] And the Agile Manifesto is poised to help organizations transition to this new paradigm. However, because of its essentially subjective nature, different individuals interpret the manifesto differently, leading to confusion and resistance in organizations. In successfully transitioning to an agile culture, leaders need to be aware of this potential confusion and focus on agility's "soft" characteristics, such as trust, transparency, and flexibility. The successful implementation of agile methodologies depends heavily on understanding and addressing the psychological and sociological factors at play. Transitioning to an agile culture requires a significant shift in thinking. Adopting an agile mindset requires visionary leadership that supports and empowers team members to ensure their success. Agile leaders protect the team from external factors and provide the necessary resources for them to succeed. Leaders overseeing the transition to an agile culture must navigate a delicate balance between following the literal meaning of the Agile Manifesto and fostering an environment that promotes its essence resulting in innovation and adaptability. Creating an Agile culture that values collaboration, transparency, and continuous improvement results in more adaptable and innovative organizations in today's rapidly changing digital environment.

"Soft" agile characteristics

The psychology of Agile begins with an understanding of its soft characteristics, the reasons for its popularity and value. Agile approaches' success heavily depends on the individuals involved, including their skills, motivation, and communication within and between groups. Therefore, regular training, guidance, mentoring, support, and adaptability are crucial for achieving Agile success. According to Cockburn and Highsmith,[16] friendliness, talent, skill, and communication are essential for Agile success. As Agility is applied throughout the enterprise, an additional and comprehensive understanding of sociocultural and psychological factors is needed. Agile fundamentals are complemented at the enterprise level with strategy alignment, risk management, change management, and behavioral practices that add value to the enterprise.

Some of the soft characteristics of Agile include:

- Agile is personal and subjective. Agile can be interpreted and implemented in various ways, depending on personal perspectives and working styles. These individual viewpoints are shaped by one's persona, which is based on childhood experiences. As agile interpretation is susceptible

15 Unhelkar, B., *Agile in Practice: A Composite Approach*, Cutter Consortium Agile Product & Project Management Executive Report, Vol. 11, No. 1, 2010.

16 Cockburn, A., and Highsmith, J., "Agile Software Development: The People Factor", *Computer*, November 2001, pp. 131–133.

to personal biases and perceptions, awareness of those biases and the potential for ambiguity in decision-making is acknowledged in an agile workplace. To mitigate the effects of these biases and perceptions, open communication is encouraged to bring them to light and work toward resolving them. Agile leaders recognize the personal nature of agile and actively strive to leverage it in their practices.

- Agility is a culture and a mindset. Agile is not just a method; rather, it's a way of working and a culture. The Agile culture has a mindset that is not linear or easily measurable. Real work environments are complex and consist of contradictions, which are recognized by Agile leadership. Leaders actively strive to create a balance between these contradictory characteristics.
- Agility is existential. Agile is not something new, nor is it just a methodology; it's a way of life reflected in how we work. Being an innate human characteristic, agility empowers individuals to be true to themselves. In Agile, success is about completing tasks joyfully and unhurriedly. Hence, "doing" work in an agile manner is not sufficient; "happening" is just as important as "doing" in Agile. The Agile mindset places more value on the intrinsic worth of work than on just achieving a goal. Therefore, transitioning to agile is, in reality, uncovering the existential agility within us. How work is conducted assumes greater importance than what is being produced, which becomes a byproduct of the process.
- Agility is non-competitive. An Agile team is guided by shared values that encourage transparency, openness, and continuous improvement. This fosters a non-competitive work environment. In an Agile workplace, tasks are distributed and managed collectively, with each team member taking responsibility for their respective assignments and working collaboratively with others to achieve the desired results. This culture of collaboration and ownership ensures that the Agile team remains positive, supportive, and non-competitive.
- Agility is not serious. Comprehending the importance of a relaxed and non-serious environment in an agile workplace is imperative. Excessive planning and documentation can hinder the adoption of an agile mindset. Agile leaders are keenly aware of this subtle psychological factor and they introduce humor and laughter into the work culture. Humor is essential for a thriving and healthy agile workplace and it is a part of one's personality.

Agile meta-mind

The term "meta-mind" refers to the underlying thought processes that give rise to our overt thoughts and drive our actions. Understanding the agile meta-mind is essential for agile leaders to comprehend what is agile and effectively plan for a successful transformation in the workplace. While many agile ceremonies and practices can be easily implemented with the mind, a thorough understanding of the psychological foundations of agile requires careful consideration of the meta-mind. This is so because, during daily, routine work, the outer layer of the mind focuses on specific techniques. In contrast, the inner layer, the meta-mind, deals with the source of agility, which can handle uncertainty and ambiguity. While mastering specific agile techniques is crucial, grasping the agile mindset provides the rationale behind these techniques. Consequently, it becomes possible to fine-tune techniques and roles to suit the unique needs of an agile environment.

The concept of having multiple layers in our minds is a well-known psychological phenomenon. When we ask questions like "Who understands the functioning of my mind?" we are, in fact, hinting at the existence of another layer of the mind. When we answer this question by saying, "My mind understands the functioning of my mind," we end up with two distinct minds: the mind being understood and the mind that understands. This can lead to an infinite loop of minds. The premise of a meta-mind can limit this looping of minds. A meta-mind is the mind behind the mind, and acknowledging its existence provides the psychological foundation for leadership in an agile environment. These multiple mind layers also impact the multiple layers of agile in organizations, as mentioned in the last chapter of this book. The nuances of agile's psychological foundations are fascinating and go beyond logic, moving into emotions. While there may not be definitive and precise answers to questions about the meta-mind, exploring its existence is still significant.

Here are a few questions that hint at the intricacies of the agile mind and form part of the exploration of the agile meta-mind:

- The agile meta-mind wonders whether agile was used to create agile. Indeed, the agile approach, which is used to create agility, is not based on an existing formal research method. Instead, it resulted from meetings and discussions in a ski resort that led to the creation of the Agile Manifesto. Scientific endeavors typically follow an underlying research methodology, such as quantitative or qualitative research, but there is no evidence of such a method being used in the development of agility. Despite this lack of formal methodology in arriving at agile, or perhaps because of it, Agile is the most popular approach to work and has produced tremendously significant results in workplaces. The development of agility follows the anarchist theory of Feynman, which argues that there is no such thing as the scientific method and that a single methodological rule cannot be imposed upon scientific inquiry.[17] The

17 Feyerabend, Paul K., 1970, *Against Method: Outline of an Anarchistic Theory of Knowledge*, University of Minnesota Press, Minneapolis. Retrieved from the University of Minnesota Digital Conservancy, https://hdl.handle.net/11299/184649.

foundation of Agile for Agile is the innate human nature that discovered it as an approach to work.

- The agile meta-mind raises an interesting question about the development of the Agile method: would it exist if it weren't for the traditional Waterfall methodology? The Waterfall methodology is a linear and planned approach to developing solutions, but it has faced challenges in the digital world, where business environments are constantly changing. This traditional approach has struggled to keep up with the demands of a rapidly evolving world. However, Agile may not have emerged as an alternative without the planned Waterfall-based methods. Just like thinking outside the box requires a box, Agile thinking has flourished outside the planned methods' box.
- The agile meta-mind wonders whether relentlessly pursuing goals without considering the benefits of relaxed work is the root cause of failure. For ages, it has been accepted that setting and tracking goals is essential for success. However, blindly chasing these goals without allowing for the possibility of unhurried work has not been sufficiently contemplated. The traditional ways to pursue goals recklessly have led to stress, delays, and lower-quality output. Agile work environments offer relaxation and freedom by continuously refining goals based on the work produced in each iteration.
- The agile meta-mind wonders whether measuring an entity can change its behavior, specifically focusing on the metrics and measurements used in formal project management methods.[18] While these metrics were initially intended to control and track projects, it's worth considering whether they have also contributed to increased stress levels in the workplace. The "observer effect" of quantum mechanics suggests that particles can change their behavior when observed, and this concept may be relevant here. A study by Jeffreys and Lawrence[19] provides exciting insights into how projects work. According to that study, projects that didn't have estimates made by project managers had higher-quality results and were delivered sooner compared to projects that did have estimates. Agile teams are self-organized and self-managed, with rolling estimates, minimal observation, and sparse control. This lack of stringent observation and control may have contributed to the success of agile methods.
- The agile meta-mind wonders whether things can still "happen" in a workplace even if no one is actively "doing" them. It's important to note that unplanned activities can lead to significant outcomes. By carefully observing the work environment, we can see that many positive outcomes can arise simply from enjoying the work and feeling a greater

18 PMBOK of PMI, PRINCE2, BABOK of IIBA.

19 DeMarco, T., and Lister, T., 1987, *Peopleware: Productive Projects and Team*, Dorset House, New York. A fascinating experiment by *Lawrence and Jeffrey* reported in this book on the high productivity of self-estimating, self-managing teams.

sense of self-worth. However, these outcomes may not be anticipated or easily measurable, and as a result, they are often overlooked in the daily scheme of work. One key aspect of the agile approach is to protect the team from outside disruptions and allow it to thrive from within. This can lead to more outcomes based on organic and meaningful happenings.

Methods to culture

Business organizations have long utilized methods for a specific purpose – originating from the scoping and planning of work. As the business landscape becomes increasingly complex, ambiguous, and rapidly changing, there is a growing need to bring order to this reality. This is illustrated in Figure 1.1. Methods offer a conceptual and generalized representation of the approach to comprehending and managing this amorphous reality. Effective planning involves identifying what is pertinent and scoping the essential components of reality. Hence, methods are critical for organizations to comprehensively understand their surroundings and take suitable actions.

Agile is an approach that originated in software development. Unlike building a physical object such as a house or a car, software development is a more abstract process. It is not as straightforward, and the end product is not immediately measurable. Software development is more akin to an artistic

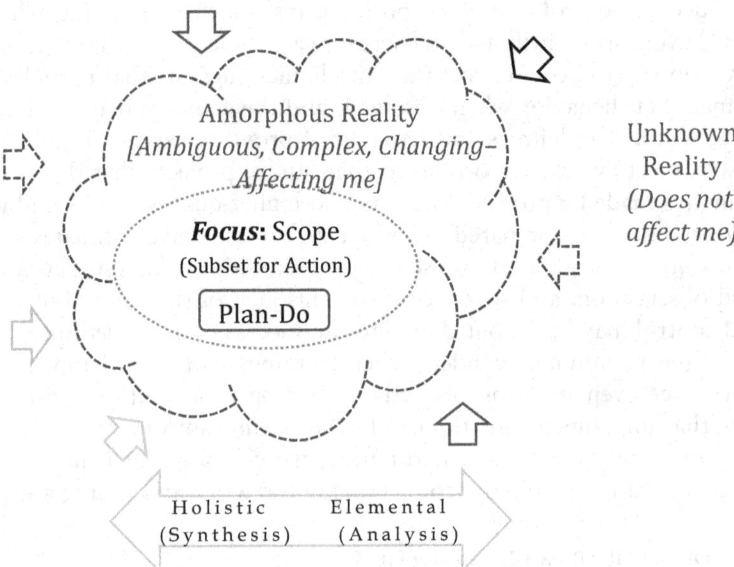

Figure 1.1 Planning Is at the End of Investigations into Amorphous Reality (Top View).

pursuit than an engineering one.[20] This is perhaps why Agile is popular in software development. Frederick Taylor's scientific management and work breakdown structure (WBS) approach is not easily applicable to software development.[21] The commonly used project management frameworks such as PMBOK and PRINCE2, techniques like WBS and Pert/CPM, and tools like MS Project, follow a linear engineering approach. However, with the increasing size, complexity, and dynamism of work, particularly in the digital age, these linear principles have resulted in failures. Lack of methods, lack of user involvement, and lack of ability to handle changing requirements have led to project failures, some of which are very well documented by Glass.[22]

Agile is an approach to work that emphasizes collaboration, iteration, and incremental progress. It has proven to be highly effective in project work due to its focus on meeting the changing needs of stakeholders. Agile techniques have been widely adopted across industries, enabling rapid product creation and immediate value for end users in software development. Today, Agile has become a cultural and leadership characteristic that promotes an iterative, incremental, and balanced approach to work. This approach can be applied to various activities, including marketing, business process optimization, and enterprise architecture design.[23]

Management to leadership

Conventional management practices tend to place significant emphasis on tasks, with a tendency to dissect problem statements into smaller, more attainable objectives. In doing so, managers may become overly focused on the completion of these tasks, rather than the ultimate value they provide. While it is crucial to identify individual roles within a project and assign tasks accordingly, this approach can fail to acknowledge the distinctive perspectives of each team member. An approach that is too rigid assumes that one developer is interchangeable with another, which does not align with the agile methodology.

The agile work environment is crafted to deliver the best possible product or service for the user. In this context, leadership plays a crucial role as agile leaders are focused on achieving successful outcomes and values. They

20 Virine, L., and Trumper, M., 2007, *Project Decisions: The Art and Science*, Management Concepts, Vienna, VA.

21 Beck, K., *Fred Taylor, Making Software, and Conversation*, Keynote address at the 34th Technology of OO Languages and Systems (TOOLS) USA 2000 Conference, Santa Barbara, CA.

22 Glass, R., 1997, *Software Runaways: Monumental Software Disasters*, Prentice Hall, Upper Saddle River, NJ.

23 Unhelkar, B., *Agile Business Analysis – Part 1 of 2 – Business Needs Exploration and Requirements Modeling in Agile Projects*, Cutter Executive Report, May 2012, USA, Vol. 13, No. 2, Agile Product and Project Management Practice.

possess the unique ability to navigate ambiguity and contradictions, acting as facilitators to bring the team together to tackle challenges. A successful Agile work environment thrives on good leadership. An exceptional leader in this setting can be compared to a catalyst in a chemical reaction. Despite their unremarkable appearance, the team feels that they are indispensable due to the psychological astuteness of an agile leader.[24]

The adoption of Agile methodology has proven to be a significant advantage for businesses, as its benefits extend beyond software development projects. Previously, corporate leaders were least interested in approaches such as Waterfall, procedural, object-oriented, or component-based and more interested in the final output. However, Agile has now become a sought-after leadership trait that business executives aim to integrate into their modeling of business functions and governance strategies in the digital age. Leadership in Agile takes a minimal planning approach and focuses on maximum facilitation. It is not a top-down approach. This acknowledgment brings subjectivity (as opposed to objective and highly metrics-driven project management) and leadership (as opposed to stringent task management) into focus. Agile's triumph can be attributed to its emphasis on individuals and ability to handle subjectivity, making it an indispensable component of project success alongside technology, data, programming, and testing.

Agile mind

The agile mindset is based on the principles of the agile meta-mind. Agile methodology was intended to help the software development community move away from the traditional approach of up-front planning, excessive documentation, and analysis paralysis. As a result, development projects became more collaborative, cross-functional, and lively, leading to the realization that agility is an innate and existential characteristic. Consequently, the business community embraced the agile mindset, and various functions such as marketing, HR, accounting, and compliance started adopting it. The adoption of the agile mindset is based on accepting that agile is a subjective approach. Daily scrums, user stories, stand-ups, Kanbans (visible charts), and other ceremonies are critical for success in an agile work style, but they provide a limited understanding of Agile's potential. Understanding the agile mindset is crucial to apply agile in the rest of the organization. The relevance of agile in operations is evident in the DevOps approach, where agile development is combined with agile deployment in operations. The Agile mindset is the true differentiator between traditional planned methods

24 "Characteristics of an Agile Leader," *PremierAgile*. Available at: premieragile.com/characteristics-of-agile-leader/#:~:text=An%20Agile%20leader%20such%20as,grows%20as%20a%20better%20individual (Accessed: 14 July 2023).

and the flexibility required in the modern digital era. While agile ceremonies may be attractive, the underlying mindset is even more so.

Based on the agile meta-mind, the agile mindset is an essential toolkit for any agile leader. It is the foundation for applying agility in practice. An agile leader makes things happen and is willing to adapt to changes that may arise. The agile mindset is bold in accepting that not everything will go according to plan and that sometimes, plans themselves may not be necessary. Balancing planning and non-planning is a critical contribution of agile leadership. The agile mindset also acknowledges the individualistic nature of Agile. Psychosocially astute agile leadership is highly sensitive to an individual's psychological makeup, their early childhood experiences, personal fears, aspirations, and dynamics within a group. Agile leadership is acutely aware of the variety of personalities in a group or organization and accepts the differences rather than rejecting them.

Understanding psychological frameworks and how they affect individuals and groups is a crucial skill for agile leaders. Every interaction within an agile team is influenced by the mental baggage carried by each member. Agile leaders must recognize biases in decision-making, including their own, that may stem from their overall personality. In the subsequent chapters of this book, the transactional analysis (TA) framework is introduced to assist in team formation and group dynamics. Theories related to right and left-brain dominance, thinking speed, and Maslow's hierarchy, along with the Myers–Briggs Type Indicator (MBTI) and the CAMS, are all part of an agile mindset.

BE-HAPPEN VERSUS PLAN-DO

As organizations adopt the agile mindset, individuals experience a sense of freedom and elation at work. This leads to increased creativity and productivity at all levels – individual, team, and organizational. The agile way of work is based on trust, simplicity, and collaboration, alleviating stress and fostering creativity.

Figure 1.2 illustrates the three aspects of work within an organization – "Plan-Do," "envision-evolve," and "Be-Happen." The latter refers to an existential leadership approach at work that is highly productive and is also discussed in a later chapter on agile transformations. The agile work style can be intriguing to someone rooted in the traditional "planning and doing" mindset. It is important to understand the innate, existential nature of agile, which is recognizing that individuals can "be" as they are. This realization by the leaders of letting people "be" produces another intriguing result: "happening." The philosophy of an agile work environment is not just about "Plan-Do." It is also about "Be-Happen". The "Be-Happen" philosophy is vital to Agile, as it is ideally suited for those who enjoy their work and are not pressured by deadlines, documentation, or deliveries. In

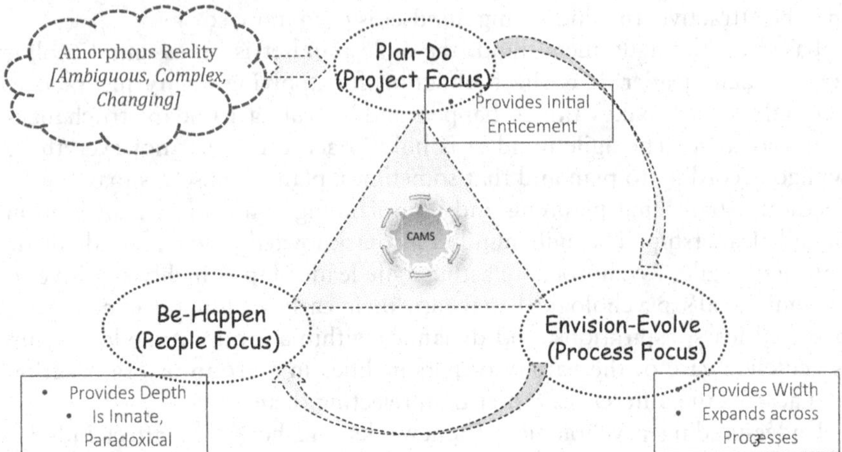

Figure 1.2 Agile Leads to a Quantum Jump: From "Plan-Do" (Project Focus) to "Be-Happen" (People Focus).

an Agile culture, the focus is on delivering honest, high-quality work that leads to greater productivity and team satisfaction. A substantial amount of agile work occurs organically, and good agile leaders ensure they step out of the way of a team producing such work.

Individualistic agile

It can be risky to allow a worker to "be" rather than constantly "doing" things unless the individualistic nature of agile psychology is properly understood. At its core, agile is all about the individual. Agile environments provide individuals freedom from the bureaucratic pressures of formal, planned environments, allowing them to work as they see fit. However, in such an environment, individual motivations and biases can significantly impact the team's overall work. Therefore, every member of an agile team must be aware of their own biases and be ready to accept them. The psychology of Agile emphasizes the importance of understanding individual natures so that they can work together as a team.

Analysis and synthesis

Leaders often face complex problems that require breaking down into smaller, more manageable tasks. This process is called analysis. It helps to understand the problem in detail, leading to task-oriented solutions. The output of this analysis is a WBS – a list of tasks with assigned resources.

However, analysis alone is not enough. It's equally important to take a holistic view of the situation and consider how these individual tasks fit together. This is where synthesis comes in. Synthesis involves combining multiple tasks into a synchronized whole, which is crucial for successful execution. Even if all the parts are well analyzed, they may not fit together as intended without proper synthesis.

Analysis helps identify the components that need to be synthesized. While analysis is essential for understanding a problem, synthesis is the key to executing a successful solution. By breaking down a problem into its components and then synthesizing those components into a cohesive whole, it's possible to manage complexity and achieve success.

Given the tremendous importance of synthesis in holistic agile work, this topic is revisited in the chapter on agile transformations.

PSYCHOSOCIOLOGY OF AGILE: ENCOMPASSING INDIVIDUAL, GROUP, ORGANIZATION, INDUSTRY, AND SOCIETY

Figure 1.3 illustrates how five interconnected aspects of psychosociology impact individuals, groups, organizations, industries, and societies. Although psychology is relevant to all of these levels, its application varies depending on

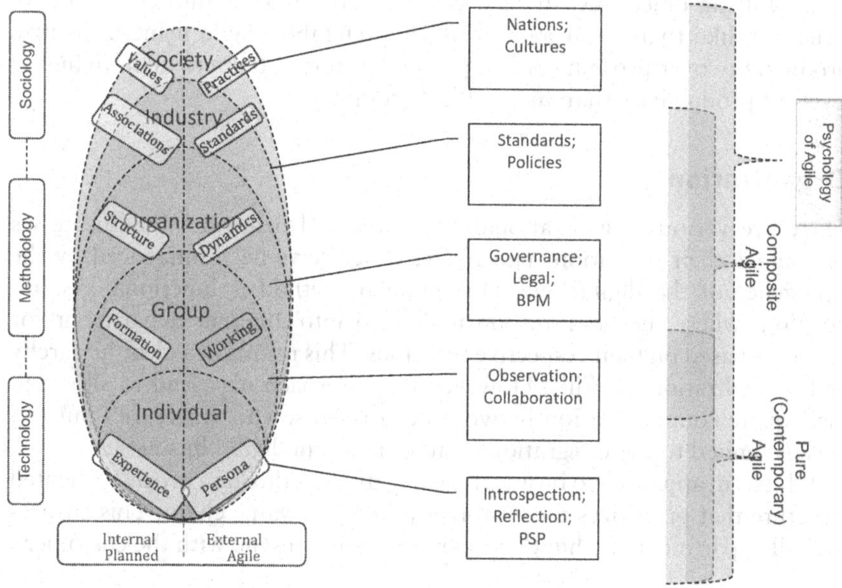

Figure 1.3 Individual, Group, Organization, Industry, and Society: Psychology of Agile.

the specific aspect. Each psychological aspect is made up of an internal facet that originates from structured and deliberate methodologies, and an external facet that originates from agile methodologies. In the following paragraphs, there is a brief explanation of each of these facets.

Individual

Our inner world influences our thoughts, while our outward behavior shapes how we interact with others. To successfully navigate group dynamics, it's crucial to reflect on our experiences and their impact on those around us. This introspection is a fundamental aspect of the Agile practice of "retrospective." Despite time constraints, we can still engage in self-reflection and personal growth in all areas of our lives. Each honest reflection offers insights into (1) our own experiences and (2) how our behavior affects those around us. These insights are indispensable for fostering effective group dynamics and personal development.

Group

Collaborating with a group requires consideration of multiple factors. The team's structure and dynamics vary as each member contributes their unique perspective.[25] While a hierarchical structure with strict reporting lines can be effective for established goals, it may not be the best approach for initiatives with evolving objectives. In such cases, a more flexible and collaborative structure, like that of an agile team, is preferable. Agile teams prioritize productivity over procedures and policies, allowing them to achieve higher levels of productivity than hierarchical groups.

Organization

There are various organizational structures and behaviors for businesses to manage their operations effectively, which have been influenced by the emergence of the digital age. One popular method is functional decomposition, where the organization is divided into different departments or divisions based on their respective functions. This results in a clear hierarchy and specialization of skills. However, this approach may lead to silos and inadequate communication between departments. This structure's importance is limited to the integration of automation in digital business.

A different approach to business organization is utilizing a process-oriented structure that prioritizes the customer journey or value chain. This ensures that all departments within the organization are in sync with the customer's

25 Berne, E., 1984, *The Structure & Dynamics of Organizations and Groups*, Ballantine Books, New York, NY.

needs and objectives. However, this approach can be more intricate to manage due to its complexity. An effective method of customer-oriented design is business process reengineering (BPR), which Michael Hammer and James Champy[26] introduced in the 1990s. BPR involves reassessing business processes from the ground up to eliminate waste, enhance efficiency, and deliver better customer service. With the help of digital technologies that enable data-driven decision-making, customer-facing process-oriented structures and behaviors can be supported.

Another option is a flattened or collaborative organizational structure. This approach involves fewer management layers and a greater emphasis on teamwork and collaboration. While it can lead to quicker decision-making and increased innovation, it can be difficult to implement in larger organizations due to the need for self-ownership and self-organization.

Finally, mixed or matrix structures combine elements of the above approaches, such as a functional decomposition with cross-functional teams or a process-oriented structure with a clear reporting structure. This can help balance the benefits and drawbacks of different approaches but can also be more complex to manage.

The modern economy places a high value on customer satisfaction, and digital technologies and AI are accelerating changes in organizational structures. The emergence of advanced cloud computing and business analytics is creating exciting opportunities for innovative approaches to organizational behavior. AI-powered tools and platforms, in particular, offer businesses the ability to analyze customer data in real time, enabling more dynamic and responsive organizational design. Flexibility is crucial for achieving agile organizational design, allowing businesses to adapt quickly to changing market conditions and customer needs.

Industry

Industries consist of various organizations operating within a shared market or supply chain. To ensure smooth operation within this group, it's essential to establish a set of standards and policies to guide their actions. The ability to swiftly adapt to unforeseen circumstances is a crucial factor in developing these guidelines and ultimately determines the success of each organization within the industry. Agility plays a significant role in helping industry groups define their boundaries, identify their dominant economic characteristics, and focus on their core activities. This focus is particularly vital during unprecedented events like the recent COVID-19 pandemic. Additionally, industry groups can exert a significant impact by forming powerful lobby groups that collaborate to challenge governing bodies. Agility is the most

26 Hammer, M., and Champy, J., 1993, *Reengineering the Corporation: A Manifesto for Business Revolution*, HarperBusiness, New York.

critical trait for an industry to survive. A rigid, procedure-bound industry group would struggle to adjust to rapidly changing, uncertain, and unpredictable environments. Therefore, it's crucial for industry groups to embrace agility and adaptability to remain relevant and resilient in the face of shifting circumstances.

Society

Agility has the potential to become a significant social value, but it must be balanced with planning. This balance affects individuals, teams, organizations, and entire industries, and has a profound impact on society as a whole. The rise of digital organizations has caused a shift in societal values and priorities, as digital technologies transform various aspects of our lives. The accessibility and widespread use of these technologies have changed social practices such as community building, value-seeking, and understanding of one's rights and responsibilities. As a result, social values and practices are evolving to better align with the structure and dynamics of the digital world.

Technology–methodology–sociology

A successful work project requires a balanced use of agile methods that consider the trilogy of technology, methodology, and sociology. While the technology used for development and project management heavily influences outcomes, the development methodology employed is equally important. Linear, Waterfall-based approaches may lead to different results than iterative, incremental ones. Understanding the reasons for project failures requires careful consideration of the "what, how, and who" of managing work. For instance, personalized mobile devices brought in under the label of Bring Your Own Device (BYOD)constitute the "what," while policies and procedures on how to use these devices within the organization's firewalls make up the methodology. Sociology encompasses the protocols, ethics, and personal use of those who work there. At the organizational level, technology refers to cloud computing, methodology refers to the business processes that utilize the cloud, and sociology considers the impact of the cloud on employee work and end-user interaction with the organization. To balance technology, methodology, and sociology, careful leadership and a focus on creating a productive work environment are necessary.

COMPOSITE AGILE METHOD AND STRATEGY (CAMS)

Agile leadership requires a delicate balancing act, with success hinging on a deep understanding of psychology and a keen avoidance of extremes. One such extreme is the choice between planned methodologies and pure agile approaches. The former emphasizes tools, documentation, contracts, and resistance to change, while the latter prioritizes people, their interactions, working solutions, collaboration, and adaptability. To achieve optimal results, a balanced, composite approach is required. This section underscores the significance of achieving this equilibrium.

Composite agile

When it comes to Agile leadership and coaching, finding the right balance is key. Robert Galen has identified two groups of Agilists[27]: purists and pragmatists, and he considers himself part of this spectrum. Neither approach is inherently flawed, but how leaders put agility into practice and guide their teams can make a significant difference. To create a truly effective Agile culture, it's important to combine structure and flexibility, technology and psychosociology. This balancing act is known as composite Agile. The CAMS is a strategic approach to fostering a harmonious workplace that blends planned and agile ceremonies, roles, and deliverables, while also achieving balance between the two aspects of the Agile Manifesto.

Agile methodology is not a one-size-fits-all solution and can vary depending on the specific project and organizational culture. While some practitioners may be strict in their adherence to the methodology, others take a more practical approach that draws on their experience and situational awareness.[28] Successful Agile practitioners prioritize understanding their clients' perspectives and avoid setting unrealistic expectations. The CAMS framework promotes cross-training in multiple work areas to create well-rounded Agile practitioners. The Pragmatic Agile philosophy finds a balance between planning and adaptability while staying true to the core values of Agile methodology. This approach is embodied in the CAMS model.

As illustrated in Figure 1.3 to the right, Agile development methodologies such as Scrum and XP hold tremendous potential for individuals and small teams, while composite Agile offers even greater benefits for organizations and entire industries. Delving into the psychology behind Agile can have wide-ranging implications for society at large. The core principles of Agile center around shared goals and an unending pursuit of growth and advancement in small increments, often referred to as Kaizen.

Agile culture and Yin-Yang

Achieving success in an agile culture requires a delicate balance that can only be maintained through awareness, mindfulness, and a deep understanding

27 Galen, R., "Selecting an Agile Coach: Critical Considerations P2," *Project Times*, 4 September 2013. Available at: www.projecttimes.com/robert-galen/selecting-an-agile-coach-critical-considerations-p2.html.

28 www.pmi.org/learning/library/blending-agile-waterfall-successful-integration-10213.

of the complexities involved. While the flexibility of Agile has proven to be beneficial, proper planning and formal tracking of work remain critical. This is where the practical concept of Yin-Yang comes into play, where opposing elements must coexist in harmony.[29] Agile leaders understand that leadership style is influenced by both individual and organizational culture. Each industry and organization has its unique way of doing things, which is subject to interpretation. Therefore, what works for one organization may not apply to another. For example, governmental organizations, known for their extensive bureaucracies, tend to have a culture of excessive documentation. In such settings, agility leans heavily toward documentation. On the other hand, some workplaces have a more visual and open culture, where less documentation and more informal communication based on trust is encouraged. Each cultural background presents unique opportunities for individuals to thrive.

Agile methodology emphasizes acknowledging the psychological complexity of competing demands in the workplace. Leaders at all levels, whether overseeing a project or an entire organization, work to establish a social and cultural atmosphere that can accommodate these contradictions. Although Agile promotes innovative and flexible approaches, it can also lead to disruptions. A truly adept leader can seamlessly integrate the opposing forces of freedom and discipline – the complementary elements of Agile.

To effectively manage a project, it's crucial to strike a balance between planned and Agile approaches that take into account the project's unique requirements and limitations. The key is to find the sweet spot between detailed planning and flexibility, considering factors such as project complexity, importance, team dynamics, and external influences. Before implementing Agile methodology, leaders should assess their team's capabilities and needs and any constraints imposed by external factors. By combining both approaches, a well-defined framework can be established that adapts to changes seamlessly. While Agile methodology helps prevent mistakes and increase visibility, the iterative and incremental nature of the approach carries risks such as insufficient documentation and estimations. Achieving a balance between structure and collaboration requires continuous monitoring and adjustments.

Carl Jung's psychological process of integrating opposites to gain a comprehensive perspective of reality laid the foundation for numerous frameworks such as the popular MBTI personality tests. Chapter 3 of this book explores these psychological frameworks in the context of agile at work.

Taking a comprehensive approach means considering all the systems involved in a project, rather than just one part of it. For example, SAFe[30]

29 Unhelkar, B., 2015, *The Psychology of Agile-II: Group Dynamics and Organizational Adoption*, Cutter Executive Report, Oct 2015, Vol. 16, No. 4, Boston, USA.

30 Leffingwell, D., 2017, *SAFe Reference Guide: Scaled Agile Framework for Lean Software and Systems Engineering*, Addison-Wesley, Boston, MA.

provides a comprehensive approach for large-scale projects that require both Agile methodologies. By working closely with the product owner and prioritizing impactful tasks, better results can be achieved. A key factor in achieving this balance is creating a culture of thoughtful and deliberate decision-making. A workplace that encourages this approach is better able to determine when planning and documentation are necessary versus when flexibility and open dialogue are needed. A comprehensive and holistic approach to work requires a balanced work culture, which in turn leads to less pressure and increased flexibility. Balance is essential for achieving a stress-free workplace, which is well positioned to deliver high-quality work.

Yin-Yang promotes effective leadership by skillfully balancing efficiency and effectiveness. Agile leadership fosters a culture of focus among all team members, ensuring that the most crucial tasks are tackled at the right time. By showcasing strategic planning and clear objectives on a visible board, a thoughtful and balanced view of ongoing work is presented. This transparency facilitates workload redistribution and prevents burnout, ensuring a harmonious and productive work environment. Achieving effective Agile leadership entails a continuous process of balancing opposing forces and prioritizing practical delivery. The ability to seamlessly integrate these opposing forces is a critical aspect of Agile leadership. For instance, even though the first user story may be displayed on a wall for all to see, some documents and requirements may not be as easily visible. Agile leaders must consider the diverse personalities on their team, some of whom may be comfortable with the wall display approach while others may not. To address this, it may be necessary to introduce the latter group to the Agile culture or provide alternative opportunities that align with their working style. By employing the right tools and processes, a well-rounded and harmonious work culture can be established.

CONSOLIDATION WORKSHOP

1. What is the significance of considering the psychology and sociology of Agile? What could be the consequences if a leader neglects these aspects of Agile?
2. Can you provide some examples of the difference between leadership and management? Additionally, could you explain why leadership is more crucial than management in an Agile environment?
3. Can you explain what a meta-mind is? Could you also discuss the meta-mind of Agile and how it contributes to a better comprehension of the psychology of Agile?
4. Please provide examples and thoughts on the concept of whether events would occur if there were no individuals causing them. This should be discussed in relation to the "Plan-Do" versus "Be-Happen" psychology of Agile.

5. Could you elaborate on the differences between the "method" and "culture" components of Agile development? It would be helpful if you could provide specific examples to illustrate your point.
6. Can you explain the distinction between analysis and synthesis? Additionally, what are the benefits associated with each term, and how can a leader apply them in real-world scenarios?
7. In what ways does Agile influence individuals, groups, organizations, industries, and societies? How can each of these entities maximize their advantages by utilizing Agile practices?
8. Discuss how a leader can best utilize the dynamic nature of Agile. In particular, explore the concept of the Yin-Yang of Agile. What would be your key criteria in bringing about balance in your team?
9. What is the trilogy of technology-methodology-sociology of Agile? Explain with answers at individual and organizational levels.

Chapter 2

The agile mind-map

Manifesto, values, principles, and practices

CHAPTER SUMMARY

This chapter delves into the core elements of Agile leadership, highlighting the importance of understanding what truly comprises Agile in order to enhance leadership effectiveness. The chapter presents a mind-map, which is a powerful tool for organizing the various aspects of agility into a clear visual. The mind-map encompasses the fundamentals, manifesto, values, principles, and practices of Agile while also clarifying what falls outside its scope. By adopting a bird's eye view, leaders can gain clarity on the scope of Agile and how to apply psychological constructs during implementation within their organization. The chapter emphasizes the need for Agile leaders to adapt their approach according to the unique culture of their team and organization, which is crucial for the successful application of Agile. Overall, this chapter provides valuable insights for Agile leaders on how to effectively understand agile concepts and techniques to enhance their leadership capabilities.

INTRODUCTION

Successful team and organizational behavior relies heavily on psychological principles. Agile methodologies place a strong emphasis on individual interactions, but these are complex and difficult to quantify. Each team member has their own unique way of operating that must align with the movements and quirks of the rest of the team. Leaders in an agile environment must have a deep psychological understanding of the methodology in order to guide their team toward effective structure and dynamics. However, this can prove challenging since there is often a gap between the defined principles of Agile and their practical application within a team. Team members and leaders may need to rely on their intuition when using Agile, which can further complicate matters.

To successfully apply Agile, it's crucial to comprehend the core values, principles, and practices detailed in the Agile Manifesto, as well as the

DOI: 10.1201/9781003201540-2

variations from those basics when practicing agility. This chapter dives into Agile's makeup by utilizing a mind-map. The visual representation will demonstrate Agile's fundamental principles, exhibit the interdependence of its various components, and provide the foundation for practical advice on implementing Agile techniques in real-world scenarios. An Agile mind-map is an invaluable tool in achieving this. It aids leaders in gaining a deeper understanding of Agile as a culture and leadership trait by organizing the various elements of Agile and their practical applications in a visual format. A successful Agile leader has a comprehensive understanding of the various dimensions of Agile and the ability to communicate that understanding when implementing the agile mindset in practice. Given Agile's adaptable and diverse nature, this chapter offers a comprehensive overview of the approach. It establishes understanding and eventual application of the elements of Agile.

AGILE MIND-MAP

A mind-map is a useful tool to gain clarity on the fundamental principles of Agile, their relation to the manifesto, and how to implement them successfully. Breaking down the complexity of Agile into smaller, more manageable components, a mind-map enables prioritization of activities, which is crucial for bringing about an agile transformation and culture change. Moreover, mind-maps promote innovative thinking and issue resolution, allowing leaders to generate a variety of creative alternatives in fostering an Agile culture. An Agile mind-map is an incredibly effective organizational and focus tool for leaders.

The mind-map shown in Figure 2.1 provides an in-depth explanation of the key components of Agility. This approach encompasses the Agile Manifesto, core values, 12 principles, and a range of techniques that are incorporated into popular methods like Scrum and XP.[1] To create an Agile work environment, all the elements depicted in the mind-map should be taken into account. The map includes cognitive, behavioral, and psychoanalytical dimensions that aid in understanding the manifesto, values, principles, and practices of Agility. Adopting an Agile mindset can enhance teamwork and change management skills for leaders. By leveraging this map, leaders can effectively facilitate and encourage the adoption of Agile practices. Understanding the cognitive, behavioral, and psychoanalytical dimensions is crucial to bringing about cultural shifts at the project and organizational levels.[2]

1 Unhelkar, B., *The Psychology of Agile: Fundamentals beyond the Manifesto*, Cutter Executive Report, Dec 2013, Vol. 14, No. 5, Agile Product & Project Management Practice, Cutter, Boston, USA.

2 Weiten, W., 2012, *Psychology: Themes and Variations*, Cengage Learning, Belmont, CA.

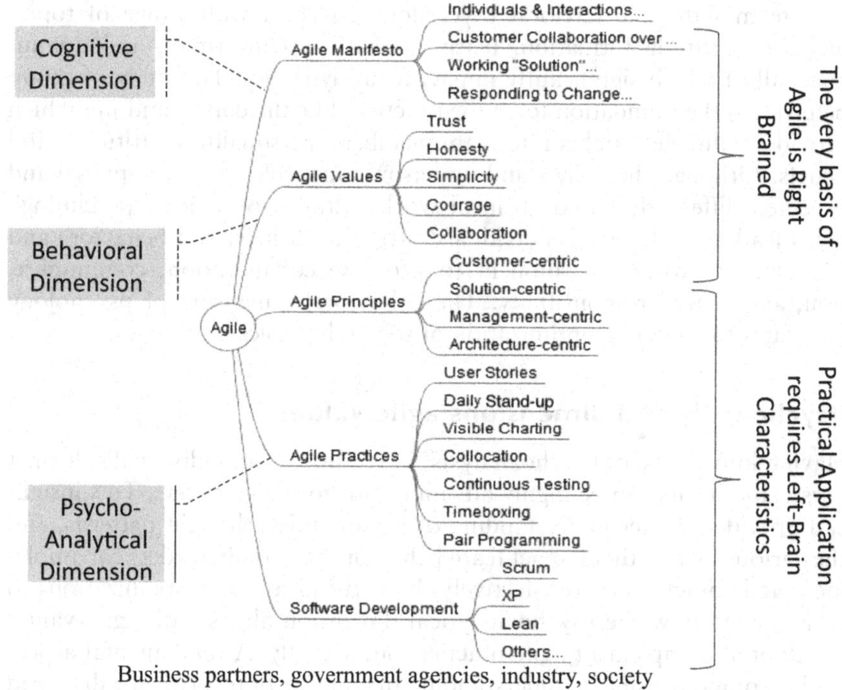

Figure 2.1 The Mind-Map of Agile (for Organizational Adoption).

Cognitive dimension of psychology and agile

Understanding the cognitive dimension is a vital component of psychology that delves into intricate mental processes such as memory, reasoning, language, problem-solving, decision-making, and creativity. Its influence on cognitive psychology is profound and has had a significant impact on the development of the Agile Manifesto. The principles set forth in the manifesto are deeply rooted in cognitive processes, offering valuable guidance for fostering an agile work culture, including flexibility, change, and trust. Leaders should regard the manifesto as a non-authoritative guide for creating a dynamic work environment. Although challenging to quantify in practice, the four manifesto statements rooted in cognitive psychology form the bedrock of agility.

Behavioral dimensions of psychology and agile

Behavioral and social psychology is the study of how social factors affect human behavior in interpersonal interactions. This field is closely related to

Agile values and principles that are essential in shaping individual behavior in a team setting. Behavioral psychology covers a wide range of topics including attitude formation, biases, prejudice, conformity, and dominance, all of which significantly impact team dynamics. The study of group behavior is the foundation for Agile practices like the daily stand-up, which provides valuable insights into team members' personalities, attitudes, and beliefs. Although the daily stand-up has minimal rules, it is interpreted and executed differently based on local work cultures. Behavioral psychology helps leaders understand individuals' attitudes, beliefs, and behaviors and fine-tune the work environment to promote collaboration, communication, and shared responsibility. The behavioral dimension of psychology facilitates the ongoing optimization of social dynamics.

Psychoanalytical dimensions agile values

Having knowledge of psychoanalysis[3] in relation to an individual's distinct personality traits can be highly advantageous for agile leaders. This insight can provide a better understanding of personalities, thought patterns, and the various factors that impact team behavior. As a result, leaders can implement agile practices more effectively. It is crucial for agile organizations to comprehend how the psychoanalytical dimension aligns with agile values to adopt and implement agile practices successfully. A fundamental aspect of this comprehension is understanding the intersection between values and motives. In a workplace, motives can drive individual actions and behaviors, while values such as trust, honesty, simplicity, and courage can unite individuals with a shared value system upheld by the group. Striking a balance between these values and motives is pivotal for establishing a cooperative and gratifying agile work environment.

Table 2.1 presents the agile ecosystem as an extension of the mind-map in Figure 2.1. Each aspect of agile is listed with its corresponding basis and psycho-social relevance for creating an agile work environment.

The practical implementation of the agile aspects presented in Table 2.1 in real-life projects and organizations is explored further.

AGILE FUNDAMENTALS

The Agile approach is centered around collaboration and communication, where small teams work closely with stakeholders in an iterative and incremental manner to achieve tangible and visible outcomes. The Agile fundamentals ensure that team members are committed to self-discipline and follow a set of practices designed to promote efficiency and flexibility.

3 Weiten, W., 2012, *Psychology: Themes and Variations*, Cengage Learning, Belmont, CA, pp. 14–19.

Table 2.1 The Agile Eco-System and Their Psychosocial Relevance

Aspect of Agile	*Basis of the Agile Aspect*	*Psycho-Social Relevance*
Agile Fundamentals	Innately human	Developing an adaptive mindset that can embrace change and effectively manage risks through incremental and iterative processes is key to cultivate effective leadership in today's ever-evolving technological landscape.
Agile Manifesto	Focus on individual	Doer is far more important than deeds; change is inevitable.
Agile Values	Right-brained, artistic Top-half of Maslow's hierarchy	The foundation of a novel social framework in team and organizational structures and behavior rests on the understanding that some valuable things cannot be quantified.
Agile Principles	The statement highlights the significance of acknowledging subjectivity in the workplace and recognizing the value of individual capabilities.	Facilitate the implementation of self-organizing teams, encourage a sense of ownership toward work, and promote a culture of continuous prioritization of tasks.
Agile and Technical Capabilities	The range of information and communication technologies that are capable of being embedded in business	These capabilities refer to the implementation of a system that allows for decentralized decision-making and knowledge sharing within an organization. This system promotes a culture of self-service and collaboration, where employees are empowered to make data-driven decisions and work together toward common business goals.
Agile Practices (Techniques)	Practices based on Agile values and principles	Agile practices are best acquired through practical implementation in the workplace. The refinement and mastery of these practices are achieved through guidance, coaching, and teamwork.
Agile Processes	Agile principles and practices embedded in business processes (especially digital processes)	Agile processes embrace change and encourage its adoption by leveraging agile practices. The use of data-driven and tool-enabled solutions facilitates the evolution of business processes toward agility and efficiency.

(continued)

Table 2.1 (Cont.)

Aspect of Agile	*Basis of the Agile Aspect*	*Psycho-Social Relevance*
Agile Alignment	Continuous monitoring of conflicts at individual and method levels	Alignment is a crucial process that involves grasping the stakeholder conflicts that arise due to personal goals, and the friction caused by different methods employed within an organization. It is essential to ensure that all the stakeholders are aligned with the overall objectives of the organization, and their individual goals are in sync with the organization's mission. The alignment process is critical to optimize the organizational outputs and enhance the efficiency of the overall system.
Agile Business	Industry demands; high risks in the digital world	By sharing responsibilities, customers and business partners are integrated in decision-making and risk reduction.
Agile Composite	Practical agile is not pure agile	It is essential to maintain a balance between planned elements and Agile while approaching work strategically. However, it is important not to disregard the planned elements altogether in pursuit of Agile methodologies, as they may still hold significant value. In other words, one must not throw out the baby with the bathwater.
Agile Culture	Non-competitive, effortlessness, unhurried	Move to a mindset that accepts and enables a natural way of working: "Be-Happen."
Agile Leadership	Facilitative, non-directive, relaxed	Adopting a new mindset that emphasizes leading by example and building trust by being a "servant-leader" is essential for Agile leadership. Developing a leadership style that prioritizes the needs of team members and empowering them rather than imposing authority and control. Leaders can foster a culture of collaboration and innovation, which can help teams organizations thrive and succeed. Embracing this mindset requires understanding of the technical nuances involved in leading by example and building trust, and the ability to apply them effectively in a variety of settings.

Table 2.1 (Cont.)

Aspect of Agile	*Basis of the Agile Aspect*	*Psycho-Social Relevance*
Agile Industry	Collaboration with business partners, government agencies, industry, society	In digital organizations, continuous collaboration among various entities is common. This electronic collaboration aims to enhance business offerings and optimize processes. However, this porous nature of digital organization's boundaries raises the need for ensuring governance, risk management, and compliance measures across the industry.

These principles align with natural human tendencies and encourage adaptation and the acceptance of change. Understanding the psychology of Agile is crucial for leaders to implement the Agile fundamentals successfully. However, implementing this approach requires a significant mindset shift among all team members. Moving from a rigid "plan-and-execute" mentality to a more relaxed and facilitative "be-and-happen" approach requires an understanding of the psychological astuteness inherent in the Agile approach.

AGILE MANIFESTO

The widely recognized Agile Manifesto defines Agile as a set of values rather than a set-in-stone plan or procedure, providing the groundwork for Agile values, principles, and practices. This manifesto serves as the framework for all Agile methodologies and approaches, developed by seasoned methodologists with the objective of overcoming the constraints of structured phases and outputs in project management. It is beneficial to revisit the four declarations of the Agile Manifesto related to software development projects:

- *Individuals and interactions over processes and tools*
- *Working software over comprehensive documentation*
- *Customer collaboration over contract negotiation*
- *Responding to change over following a plan*

The Agile Manifesto prioritizes the first part of its four value declarations, which de-emphasizes formal estimation and prioritization techniques, standardized documentation templates, and detailed task sequencing in agile development. On the other hand, the latter part of the statements in the manifesto are more aligned with traditional Software Development Life Cycle (SDLC) or Waterfall-based methodologies, which mandate extensive planning, documentation, and modeling.

The manifesto seeks to achieve a harmonious blend of agility and traditional methodologies through a deliberate trade-off between four distinct pairs of elements. Later in this chapter and throughout the book, we will delve into the Composite Agile Method and Strategy (CAMS), a highly nuanced approach based on the psychological traits of the human mind that often oscillate between two extremes.

Agile values

The principles of the agile approach are grounded in a set of core values that embody trust, collaboration, facilitation, value focus, transparency, courage, self-organization, unhurriedness, and learnability. When an organization adopts an agile mindset, these values permeate every facet of the business. While IT functions typically become more agile, HR activities like staff development, recruitment, and training also adopt an iterative and incremental approach. Using a Kanban system increases visibility in product development and deployment, and processes become more customer-centric, straightforward, and trustworthy. Policies, procedures, and documentation are streamlined to meet minimum requirements. Leaders who embrace these agile values recognize that they are the foundation of everything agile – the framework, the method, and the culture. These values are interconnected, so embracing one naturally leads to the manifestation of others. For example, embracing unhurriedness fosters self-organization as team members have the time to organize their work. Leaders strive to instill positive changes in the organizational value systems that positively impact employees, managers, customers, business partners, and the industry.

Agile principles

The Agile principles are based on the Agile fundamentals and values. There are 12 principles, each with a psychosocial perspective that aligns with the manifesto. These principles are discussed in the following section.

1. *Customer satisfaction:* For any business, it is crucial to provide customers with value. To achieve this, it is necessary to engage in consistent and meaningful conversations with customers and internally. Agile approach prioritizes customer satisfaction over contractual delivery and promotes a collaborative approach that involves frequent feedback and continuous improvement. Compared to traditional, planned methods, agile approach reduces inflexibility. Furthermore,

reducing the time between identifying requirements and achieving desired outcomes enhances customer satisfaction by making the release visible to the customer early in the development lifecycle. By embracing rapid changes and anticipating them, the team can pivot their mindset and achieve the highest level of customer satisfaction.

2. *Acceptance of changes:* Agile encourages change and incorporates it as a crucial aspect of software development. The entire process of development and deployment is broken down into small increments to facilitate change. By embracing change, Agile enables organizations to rapidly respond to evolving customer needs, ultimately leading to better business outcomes. This methodology emphasizes iterative development, short feedback loops, and cross-functional teams, all of which facilitate the rapid delivery of high-quality software that caters to customers' changing requirements.
3. *Frequent delivery:* In an agile work environment, the timely delivery of solutions is crucial for success. Shorter delivery times mean faster feedback, which can help identify potential failures sooner. The concept of "failing fast" is important in this context, as it allows for more efficient solutions and prevents wasted time and resources. By enabling more frequent testing and refinement, quicker delivery times ultimately lead to a superior end product or a quicker identification of any issues.
4. *Collaboration between business and developer:* Collaboration is a crucial principle in developing successful solutions. It enables a collective understanding of the business problem and the most appropriate solution to resolve it. Unlike relying solely on written contracts, a collaborative approach empowers individuals to comprehend the implicit meanings and contexts behind the business requirements. Collaboration helps in gaining a deeper understanding of the problem context, which results in effective problem-solving.
5. *Self-motivation of individuals:* The key to cultivating a thriving Agile work environment lies in having driven and self-reliant individuals who are supported by their leaders in achieving their goals. This approach eliminates the need for managers to engage in excessive planning and task monitoring, as adept team members demonstrate the emotional maturity necessary to take on self-motivation and drive productivity and quality. The ability to self-motivate is invaluable in forming collaborative and cross-functional teams that can effectively operate with minimal supervision.
6. *Face-to-face conversation:* In order to promote effective communication, it is crucial to establish a common understanding of the contexts, issues, and objectives among stakeholders. Face-to-face discussions are the most effective way to communicate information, minimize misunderstandings, and decrease errors in project deliverables. Agile work environments place a premium on in-person conversations

since they facilitate prompt clarifications and follow-up inquiries, which improve communication and reduce the need for revisions. Furthermore, when stakeholders have in-person conversations, it is simpler to assess and adjust to individuals' psychosocial personalities, as outlined more comprehensively in Chapters 3 and 4.

7. *Working software (solution):* The Agile approach for software development prioritizes delivering a functional solution at each iteration, leading to a final product that is fully working at each stage of its incremental development. The iterative testing process guarantees the functionality of the product at every stage. Unlike the traditional Waterfall approach involving extensive planning, modeling, and architecture development, Agile ensures a functional solution. Integrating the functional slice of the solution with operational (also called nonfunctional) requirements leads to a more widely accepted end product. This Agile principle extends beyond software development and applies to any solution (product or service) developed by an organization.
8. *Sustainable development:* In today's Agile development landscape, practitioners adopt an incremental and sustainable methodology to build software. This approach promotes a well-rounded work-life balance by steering clear of arduous, extended work hours. It is rooted in the Agile value of composure, which minimizes workplace friction and mitigates unwarranted emotional and mental strain. Sustainable development is an effective technique that facilitates measured, top-notch work, which minimizes the need for rework and is more likely to gain stakeholder approval.
9. *Technical excellence:* The concept of technical excellence is closely tied to self-organization, as it empowers individual team members to take full responsibility for their work. By emphasizing technical excellence, team members strive to achieve exceptional and high-quality development results. With a solid technical foundation and self-motivation, team members can create solutions that are readily embraced by stakeholders. If a solution falls short of expectations, team members can rely on their courage (an essential agile value) to start fresh and produce a superior outcome. Technical excellence fosters a bottom-up approach to quality and experimentation rather than just patching up solutions. Digital technologies, such as Generative AI, are particularly advantageous in fostering technical excellence. They assist developers in creating enhanced designs, experimenting with code, conducting frequent tests, and integrating customer feedback, all in pursuit of the best possible outcomes.
10. *Simplicity in design:* One of the core tenets of agility is to prioritize a simple and clear system design, even if the final product may become more intricate. This is because complex systems are never created

from the beginning. By starting with straightforward designs, the emphasis remains on the overarching context and the benefits that the solution will provide to users. A simple design allows for the abstraction of the solution and prevents getting bogged down in complexity. Additionally, this approach enables end users and customers to provide more effective feedback, as they can more readily comprehend and interact with the solution.

11. *Self-organized teams:* Self-organizing teams thrive when team members are self-motivated and take pride in their technical expertise. Implementing sustainable practices in the work environment can enhance the benefits of self-organization even further. These teams can work together seamlessly toward a common goal with minimal supervision. However, achieving this level of spontaneous alignment requires psychological maturity from all stakeholders. With minimal internal oversight, management can instead focus their efforts on facilitating team success. Additionally, the increased trust among team members further fuels motivation for success, driving them to meet business expectations. It is intriguing to consider the possibilities of such "Utopian" teams.[4]
12. *Reflection:* Achieving agility requires the continuous collaboration and utilization of resources, including people, processes, and technologies. To maintain this, it's essential to frequently review and assess the team's working style. In agile, this practice is embedded in ceremonies like "retrospectives." Reflecting on what worked well and what could be improved in each iteration allows for fine-tuning and necessary adjustments. It also calls for a thorough analysis of previous project constructs such as architecture, design, and functionality to optimize and integrate into current processes for better results. However, this principle of reflection can only be successful if leaders in an agile work environment ensure that all individuals feel secure, comfortable, and confident. Thus, the psychology of agility plays a critical role in ensuring this.

Agile principles – Contextual groups for easy understanding and application

- To aid in the understanding and implementation of Agile principles, they have been organized into four distinct categories, as illustrated in Figure 2.2. This classification is particularly advantageous for Agile

4 Constantine, L., 1995, *Constantine on Peopleware*, Yourdon Press, Upper Saddle River, NJ; Constantine, L., Panel on "Soft Issues and Other Hard Problems in Software Development," *OOPSLA'96*, San Jose, CA, USA, Oct 1996.

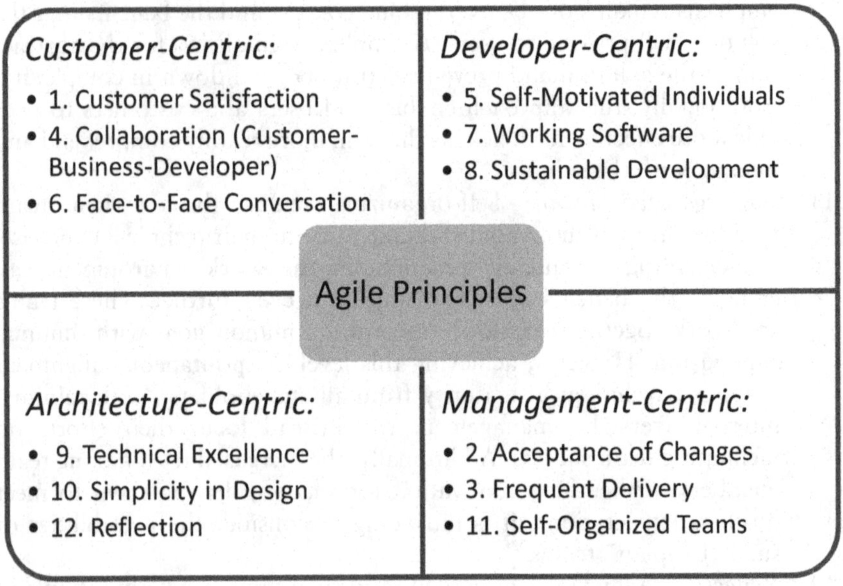

Customer-Centric:
- 1. Customer Satisfaction
- 4. Collaboration (Customer-Business-Developer)
- 6. Face-to-Face Conversation

Developer-Centric:
- 5. Self-Motivated Individuals
- 7. Working Software
- 8. Sustainable Development

Agile Principles

Architecture-Centric:
- 9. Technical Excellence
- 10. Simplicity in Design
- 12. Reflection

Management-Centric:
- 2. Acceptance of Changes
- 3. Frequent Delivery
- 11. Self-Organized Teams

Figure 2.2 Contextual Groups of Agile Principles.

leaders as it allows them to comprehend the correlation between different Agile principles in a practical environment. Additionally, these four contextual groups of Agile principles serve as a valuable memory aid for leaders, team members, and business stakeholders during their practical application.

- *Customer-centric:* These principles aim for the utmost satisfaction for end users by optimizing the benefits they derive from the solution. These principles that prioritize the needs of customers instill a new mindset in the team where the value of the solution or "release" is determined by the customer's contentment. Although solution developers may offer clarifications, the customer holds the final say in determining the value proposition. These principles place the customer at the forefront, making them the ultimate arbitrator of any initiative's success.
- *Developer-centric:* These principles prioritize the requirements of solution developers. They aim to optimize internal team operations by delegating more authority to team members, improving efficiency and effectiveness. In an agile work setting, traditional managerial roles are eliminated, and leaders focus on facilitating teamwork by removing obstacles and shielding the team from external distractions. These principles promote

creativity among developers and empower leaders to keep their teams protected from external influences.

- *Architecture-centric:* The principles of architecture-centric design provide a solid foundation for improving the quality and efficiency of a solution. These principles are crucial in crafting exceptional solution designs and architectures. They encourage analytical reasoning, architectural expertise, a forward-thinking outlook, and strategic relevance of the solution within the organization while also considering potential risks, particularly in cybersecurity.
- *Management-centric:* Although management-centric principles are typically associated with managers, they can be adopted by team members and leaders at all levels of an organization to enhance work efficiency. These principles prioritize business values and streamline management activities, resulting in improved leadership skills. However, successful implementation requires a psychologically astute mindset.

AGILE AND TECHNICAL CAPABILITIES

The success of an organization hinges on the leadership skills of its leaders at all levels, who need to possess a diverse range of capabilities encompassing both soft and agile skills, as well as technical expertise. For leaders steering digital transformations, it can be highly advantageous to have a comprehensive understanding of these agile and technical capabilities. However, embracing these skills requires a significant shift in mindset, as traditionally, leaders have tended to prioritize either technology or soft skills, but not both. A leader's ability to recognize and prioritize these varied capabilities is critical for effectively implementing agility in the workplace. Furthermore, comprehending the agile and technical capabilities within a team can serve as a sound risk-mitigation strategy. Figure 2.3 offers a concise psychological outlook on the significance of agile and technical capabilities.

Development and agility

In IT, projects are usually centered around implementing software solutions using agile development and implementation methods. Data science and Artificial Intelligence (AI) projects are such IT projects that are integral to contemporary development. These projects involve various activities, such as understanding and documenting requirements using user stories, coding and code maintenance, cloud data management, continuous testing, and working closely with multiple stakeholders. The agile approach, which is iterative and incremental, allows for regular feedback from users, thereby ensuring effective expectation management. The agile team's primary focus is to develop a solution that meets the users' needs, with the development process being merely a means to that end. When handling operational

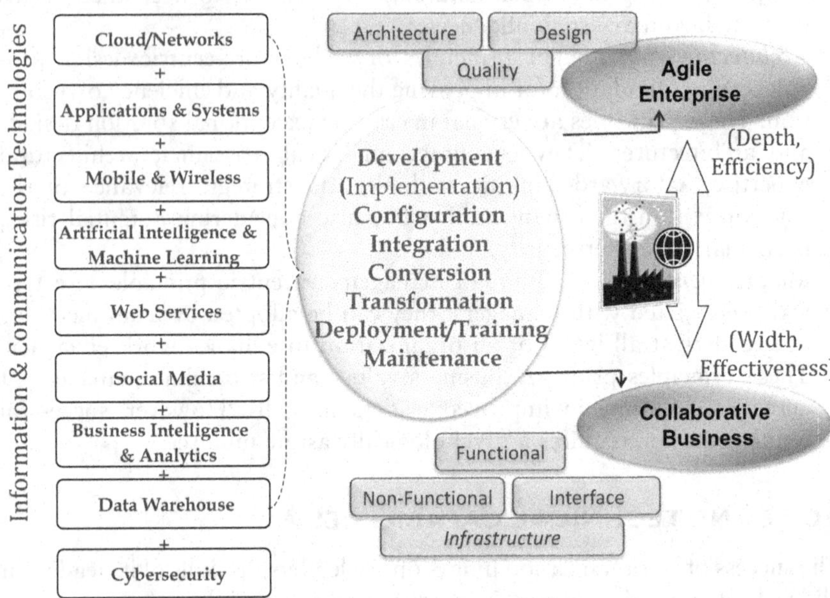

Figure 2.3 Range of Agile Capabilities (Information and Communications Technology Specific).

requirements, also referred to as non-functional requirements, such as performance, volume, scalability, and security, the composite agile approach is far more effective than the pure agile approach. This is because development using the pure agile approach does not have a mechanism for capturing these operational requirements in the user story format. The CAMS approach is highly effective in data science projects for AI-enabled solutions as it undertakes careful iterations and increments with sufficient user stories, use cases, and related documentation constructs that significantly reduce development risks.

Configuration and agility

In today's digital landscape, it's become commonplace for companies to either outsource their software development or adopt pre-existing solutions. However, integrating these third-party packages into an organization's existing framework requires meticulous configuration to ensure it meets their unique needs and provides a competitive advantage. In order to achieve this, being agile is crucial. Collaboration and open communication with business users allow for valuable insights into their processes, which can then be used to configure the solution accordingly. Continuous testing is also necessary to ensure that the configurations accurately reflect the organization's parameters and adhere to their business rules. To ensure that the solution aligns with user needs and quality requirements, it is important to thoroughly understand the requirements for configuration through business analysis and requirements modeling. This ensures the solution is tailored to meet specific needs and achieve optimal results.

Integration and agility

Integrating new software solutions with existing systems, databases, networks, and security modules is a complex process that also requires careful consideration of cybersecurity, especially when external data sources and networks are involved. To achieve optimal outcomes, integration teams should focus on technological and business goals. Critical activities such as interface modeling, pilot testing, and applying architectural constraints are essential for successful integration. Prototyping can also enhance the overall quality of the solution, even for legacy systems. Non-functional requirements are crucial in determining the success of integration. Understanding these requirements and ensuring they are met requires a certain level of psychological sophistication, as users may be unable to specify them at the start of a project. An agile work environment that allows users to gradually visualize the solution and specify increasingly refined non-functional requirements can significantly benefit integration activities.

Conversion and agility

Achieving efficient data migration in the digital world often involves converting existing data from cloud or back-end repositories to match the format of a new digital solution. This involves updating customer information, transaction histories, and existing accounts to align with new data-intensive solutions. To avoid any disruptions and time constraints, it's crucial for the conversion team to closely collaborate with business users. Agile methodologies are particularly useful in this context as they prioritize solutions that work. Technical leadership is essential to ensure data security, integrity, and compliance with non-functional requirements like availability, reliability, and cybersecurity. However, the developers' and users' mindsets are also critical contributors to successful data conversion. The conversion team must ensure that the data is consistent, accurate, complete, and conforms to the new system's specific data requirements while ensuring that users feel comfortable and secure throughout the conversion process. The success of data conversion relies on the cooperation between the conversion team and the business users, who may have psychological concerns and fears during the process. Adhering to industry standards, best practices, and compliance requirements is also critical to the data conversion process.

Transformation and agility

The effects of digital transformation are far-reaching and have an impact on multiple areas of an organization. The capabilities discussed in this section are all essential components of a successful digital transformation project. While traditional project management principles still hold true, digital transformation places a particular emphasis on Big Data stored in the cloud, the development and implementation of cutting-edge data analytical algorithms, and the integration of emerging technologies such as Generative AI. Additionally, maintaining strong cybersecurity measures is imperative, and decision-makers should rely on AI-generated insights as they make critical choices. It's important to note that the psychological implications of bias in data and analytics are also significant factors to consider in digital transformations.

Deployment, training, and agility

The deployment and training of digital technologies require a level of psychological insight that was once overlooked. The effects of automation on users and stakeholders can be profound, as individuals may feel that their talents and abilities are being replaced. As a result, it's crucial for leaders to have a thorough understanding of how to smoothly implement AI-powered data-driven decision-making systems with minimal resistance to change. Agile leaders can utilize the Kaizen approach to gradually introduce users to the new system and deliver incremental value. Furthermore, offering comprehensive user training and high-quality documentation is essential to ensure that both novice and experienced users can easily navigate the new system.

Maintenance and agility

The success of any solution depends on a continuous process of improvement and testing. Maintenance procedures are critical in managing change requests, correcting execution errors, and reducing potential risks. Maintaining digital business systems can be challenging due to their interconnectedness with other applications and dynamic databases. However, by adopting an agile approach and prioritizing simplicity, we can simplify complex data-driven systems. Creating models and documentation during the system's deployment promotes better traceability and quality during maintenance. In these situations, an agile mindset is particularly valuable as it emphasizes cooperation and consensus-based decision-making over rigid hierarchies. Regular maintenance is critical to ensure that the solution remains operational and efficient in achieving its intended objectives.

Information and communication technology capabilities

The smooth operation of business processes is made possible by the advanced capabilities of information and communications technology (ICT). These capabilities have a significant impact on an organization's day-to-day operations. To achieve optimal business outcomes, an organization must have strategic leadership, a deep understanding of the ever-evolving nature of ICT, and a steadfast commitment to adaptability. The successful implementation of ICT capabilities requires the adoption of agile values, principles, and practices. This is because agility enables effective collaboration between business users, technology experts, compliance officers, and auditors. Each agile trait has a specific impact on these capabilities. Figure 2.3 offers a concise summary of the capabilities that can be achieved by leveraging various technologies within an organization's digital infrastructure.

1. *Cloud network capability:* This feature enables an organization to dynamically adjust its ability to store and process data, test and deploy solutions, and undertake Big Data analytics. Virtualization via cloud servers facilitates agility in development and deployment.
2. *Applications and systems capability:* This feature empowers an organization to enhance its application offerings through back-end collaboration and integration using standardized interfaces. It also enables the organization to personalize its offerings to the users.
3. *Mobile and wireless capability:* This feature enables offering services and applications independently of the user's location.
4. *Artificial intelligence and machine learning capability:* This feature enhances an organization's ability to process data rapidly, make predictions, and make appropriate decisions relevant to the user context.
5. *Web services capability:* This feature enables the exchange of data and information for enhanced decision-making across various technical environments. It also allows the processing of data and information at various nodes.
6. *Social media capability:* This feature enables an organization to understand its position in the "alternative data" space and take corrective actions.
7. *Business intelligence and analytics capability:* This feature enables an organization to use available data rapidly, apply innovative analytical models to it, and generate correlations between widely dispersed data to enhance decision-making.
8. *Data warehouse capability:* This feature enables an organization to strategize for Big Data, deciding on sourcing, ingesting, analyzing, storing, and safely destroying data. Decisions to buy, rent, or freely tap into available data are a part of this capability.

9. *Cybersecurity capability:* This feature is crucial for a safe and efficient digital infrastructure. Maintaining a balance between agility and cybersecurity is important. Agility allows quick responses to threats, while cybersecurity safeguards against attacks and data breaches. Prioritizing both ensures resilience in the face of evolving challenges.

Architecture, design, and quality capability

The effectiveness of an organization's systems hinges greatly on the excellence of its architecture, design, and development. These elements are essential for producing superior outcomes and require diligent attention throughout development and upkeep. Agile methodologies promote a well-rounded approach that provides sufficient architecture and design to support iterative solution releases. Nevertheless, attaining this balance necessitates a mindset that can accept partially complete architecture or design artifacts while iterations are underway. While an organization's architecture and design are vital components of its enterprise architecture, they are crafted gradually and iteratively within an agile work setting.

Requirements (functional, non-functional, and interface) capability

In the field of Business Analysis, there are three essential types of requirements that are advocated for: functional, non-functional, and interface. These requirements are obtained through a combination of psychological understanding and modeling techniques. This process involves asking pertinent questions, digging deeper into each, and identifying the root causes of problems or opportunities. Functional requirements are especially relevant in new development projects and can be used during system maintenance to evaluate requested changes. Non-functional requirements, on the other hand, are more important when integrating or deploying systems or converting data during digital transformations to ensure cross-system integration and quality data conversion. Finally, interface requirements encompass user interfaces, system interfaces, and printer interfaces and must consider the increase in mobile device usage and various factors such as device type, location, and personalization needs.

Agile practices (techniques)

Agile methods include a set of practices and techniques that fall under an Agile framework used by organizations. The IIBA's BABOK 3.0 outlines 50 distinct techniques, many of which are rooted in Agile principles. Along with development techniques, essential leadership practices often include various techniques based on the psychology of Agile. BABOK highlights techniques such as Backlog Management, Balanced Scorecard, Brainstorming, Business

Capability Analysis, Business Rule Analysis, Collaborative Games, Concept Modeling, Data Dictionary, Data Modeling, Decision Modeling, Document Analysis, Estimation, Focus Groups, Functional Decomposition, Glossary, Interface Analysis, Item Tracking, Lessons Learned, Mind-Mapping, Non-functional Requirements Analysis, Organization Modeling, Prioritization, Process Modeling, Prototyping, Risk Analysis and Management, Root Cause Analysis, Scope Modeling, Stakeholder List, Map, or Personas, SWOT Analysis, Use Cases and Scenarios, User Stories, and Workshops, which are particularly noteworthy. To apply these techniques effectively, it is necessary to have experience in their usage as these techniques vary depending on the project, the individuals involved, and the project's level of criticality.

Agile practitioners can benefit from having job aids that depict a subset of Agile techniques used in projects. These job aids can help ease the use of agility in practice. Figure 2.4 provides a succinct representation of such job aids.

Pre-Iteration: [5], [6], [7] – these techniques are typically carried out before or at the start of an iteration.
During-Iteration: [1], [2], [3], [4], [8], [9], [12], [13] – these are techniques practice on an ongoing basis throughout the project
Post-Iteration: [10], [11] – these techniques are carried out toward the end of an iteration or a project.

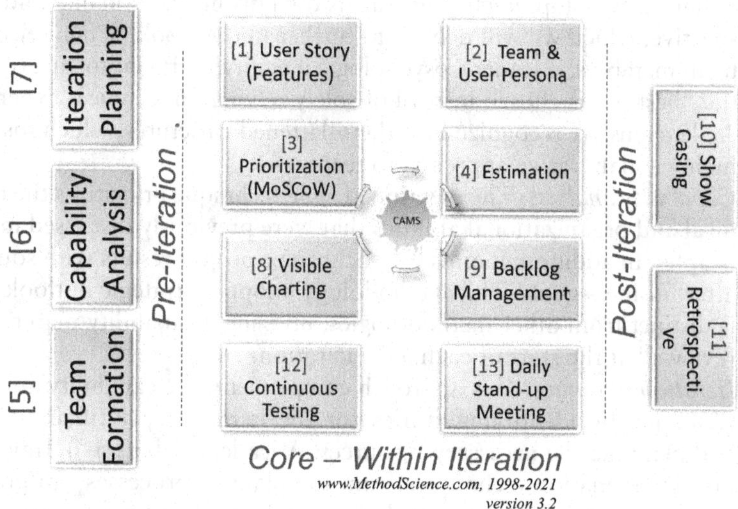

Figure 2.4 Job Aids for Agile Practices (Aligned with CAMS).

These 13 techniques are summarized in the following. Agile leaders can remember them as "job aids" in implementing and using Agile in practice.

[1] *User stories:* User stories play a crucial role in discussions as they serve as initial narratives that require further details. These stories may contain non-functional or operational specifications, including elements or activities. Usually, they are created during the initial phase of Requirements Elicitation, where both functional and non-functional requirements are gathered. It's essential to note that the author of these stories should acknowledge their preliminary nature and utilize them as a starting point for additional discussions.

[2] *Team and user persona:* The User Group Representative (Actor) profile is a lighthearted approach to depicting team members. Creating personas necessitates acknowledging team members' personalities and predispositions, which are explored further in this book. Additionally, comprehending team members' personalities is integral to conducting an effective Stakeholder Analysis.

[3] *Prioritization (MoSCoW):* In the process of iteration planning and daily stand-up meetings, the team determines priorities for user stories and other product backlog items by assigning them to one of four categories: Must, Should, Could, and Won't Have. This essential practice ensures that the team stays focused on the most critical tasks and objectives.

[4] *Estimation:* Estimating and assigning effort in user stories is a group exercise which is based on consensus rather than majority.

[5] *Team formation:* Assembling a team is a vital technique in the world of agile leadership. Each team has its own distinct personality and perspective, which we will delve into further in this book. When selecting team members, a leader's psychological acuity is crucial to ensure that the "best fit" is chosen instead of solely relying on technical expertise. Agile teams are recognized for their flattened structures, which foster a highly collaborative approach to teamwork.

[6] *Capability analysis:* The mentioned agile technique prioritizes the technical and organizational abilities that were previously discussed in this chapter. In addition, it aims to synchronize project results with sought-after business goals. This methodology adopts a strategic outlook that is distinct from other methodologies, utilizing a capability map that is reviewed at the start of each agile iteration.

[7] *Iteration planning:* This approach complements the capability analysis technique by identifying stories for the iteration, prioritizing them, and planning the necessary resources. A leader's expertise in time and budget estimation techniques from the planned processes can greatly enhance the benefits of this technique.

[8] *Visible charting:* Visual charting is a prominent method of displaying the various components involved in an iteration. The Kanban or visual board serves as a tangible representation of the user stories, tasks, team member roles, and work progress categorized into "To do, Doing, and Done" sections. However, implementing this approach requires significant emotional intelligence from the servant-leader of an agile team. It is crucial to recognize that not all team members may feel comfortable with their work and its progress being scrutinized publicly during daily stand-ups or other times throughout the day.

[9] *Backlog management:* is a technique for effectively tracking and managing work quantity during each iteration. This approach requires an agile mindset that can handle variations and anticipate changes throughout the process. Although backlog management still relies on time and resources, a skilled, agile leader understands that these units do not fully reflect each team member's potential, motivation, collaboration, and subjectivity.

[10] *Showcasing:* Demonstrating progress by displaying completed work is a successful agile technique that requires presenting the team's progress during each iteration to the product owner and business stakeholders. This procedure demands the team's commitment to crucial psychological principles, such as acknowledging constructive feedback, even if it seems unmerited, and placing user value at the forefront of all decisions.

[11] *Retrospective:* Reflecting on past performance through a Retrospective can prove to be a valuable practice for teams. It involves introspection and a deep dive into the team's performance during the iteration, with a focus on improvement rather than solely on end results. Acknowledging mistakes and committing to continuous growth are essential for a successful retrospective. Additionally, recognizing team members' unique personalities and work styles is crucial in achieving desired outcomes.

[12] *Continuous testing:* Agile methodology emphasizes continuous testing to enhance the quality of output by initiating the testing process during the product's development phase. Although certain non-functional requirements, such as performance and security, can only be fully evaluated at the conclusion of the iteration, agile team members regularly test user stories and functionalities throughout the solution development process. This approach necessitates a shift in mindset, recognizing the importance of testing partially developed products rather than solely focusing on evaluating the finished product.

[13] *Daily stand-up meeting:* The daily stand-up is a commonly used agile practice that requires team members and servant-leaders to be aware of the psychology and sociology involved in human interactions. This meeting has specific guidelines that dictate it should take place at the

same time and location every day, and last exactly 15 minutes. During the meeting, each team member must discuss what they accomplished since the last meeting, what they plan to do that day, and any obstacles they may encounter in achieving their daily goals. Paying attention to the psychological aspects is critical to ensure that the daily stand-up is not reduced to a simple status update. To ensure success, team members should remain standing, limit their discussion to the three parameters, and conclude the meeting on time. Additionally, maintaining eye contact is essential to create a sense of equality. The success of a daily stand-up depends on extensive collaboration and communication among team members.

AGILE PROCESSES

In the realm of business, models serve to illustrate the inner workings and mechanics of an organization's processes. These processes are the building blocks of an organization's tasks, outlining how activities are carried out, from customer service interactions to human resource management, sales and marketing, and the operation of machinery. With the advent of the digital age, business processes have undergone significant change, with even the most basic tasks being completed with minimal human intervention thanks to data-driven methodologies. As AI-based decision-making becomes more prevalent, these digital processes have become more complex and interconnected, necessitating the involvement of business analysts to model, analyze, and optimize these processes for maximum efficiency. The optimization of business processes requires the consideration of psychology and sociology. Stakeholders may have differing views on the criteria of necessity, efficiency, effectiveness, agility, and measurability, leading to potential conflicts in analysis. Understanding the motivations of each stakeholder becomes essential in prioritizing these processes, requiring a delicate and non-threatening approach when questioning the necessity of manual processes used by the organization in the past.

AGILE ALIGNMENT

Various methods are employed by organizations for diverse purposes, including traditional approaches such as PMBOK and BABOK, as well as auditing, process modeling, architecture, design, and testing. These techniques are used in business, governance, project management, business analysis, and development. However, the introduction of agile methods into the mix presents a challenge to the previously discussed Agile-planned dichotomy. With multiple methods operating at different levels and tiers of the organization, hidden stress can arise. Addressing the friction between these methods can significantly improve productivity and job satisfaction. Although identifying and understanding method friction can be challenging as it is invisible, examining method silos within organizations can provide opportunities to reduce friction between methods.[5] Composite agile serves as the necessary lubricant that reduces friction between methods.

AGILE BUSINESS

In the world of business, agility refers to a company's capability to respond and adapt to both internal and external changes. This ability is dependent on the organization's level of preparedness to adopt agile practices. Effective business decisions are based on a combination of analytical data and the personal experiences of decision-makers. The key components of sound decision-making include trust, collaboration, cross-functionality, intuition, iteration, visibility, and courage. These elements are precisely what define an agile business.[6] An organization's sensitivity can be measured by the time gap between a change and its response. The shorter this gap, the higher the organization's sensitivity. An organization can increase its business agility and sensitivity by reducing transactional gaps and making data-driven decisions.

AGILE COMPOSITE (CAMS)

A variety of factors, including team size, complexity, customer involvement, regulatory constraints, and risk tolerance, can impact an organization's ability to utilize agility. Effective leaders recognize these factors and strike a balance between flexibility and planning. In some instances, a combination of planned and agile methods may be necessary to leverage each approach's strengths. CAMS[7] is one such carefully designed agile approach that enables leaders to continually monitor team performance and make adjustments as needed, balancing the rigidity of planned methods with the flexibility of agile methods. Achieving this balance is an ongoing process that requires regular communication with the team and stakeholders and careful selection and modification of agile practices. Ultimately, this results in optimized internal and external business processes, leading to an inherently Agile business.

5 Unhelkar, B., *Avoiding Method Friction: A CAMS-based Perspective*, Cutter Executive Report, 20 Aug 2012, Vol. 13, No. 6, Agile Product and Project Management Practice, Boston, USA.

6 Unhelkar, B., 2013, *The Art of Agile Practice: A Composite Approach for Projects and Organizations*, CRC Press(Taylor and Francis Group/an Auerbach Book), Boca Raton, FL, USA, ISBN 9781439851180.

7 Unhelkar, B., *Agile in Practice: A Composite Approach*, Cutter Executive Report, Jan 2010, Vol. 11, No. 1, Agile Product and Project Management Practice, USA.

AGILE CULTURE

An Agile culture is one that embodies agility at all levels of the organization, integrating Agile values, principles, and practices to enable greater flexibility in decision-making. This is particularly important in the digital world, where visibility and iteration are crucial. A truly Agile culture empowers individuals at all levels to make informed decisions based on their responsibilities, with decision-making occurring across the entire organization. Data analytics is critical in enabling decentralized decision-making, providing necessary information and creating audit trails and records to support decision-making at all levels. Adopting an Agile culture requires a shift in mindset, but it is this very uniqueness that makes it so valuable.

AGILE LEADERSHIP

Agile leadership involves a fundamental change in the leader's perspective and ability to inspire individuals and teams to adopt a similar mindset. This requires agile leaders to possess strategic thinking skills that benefit the whole organization. Agile leadership is characterized by a guiding and flexible approach that is adaptable and gradual rather than prescriptive. Therefore, leaders must have a sophisticated understanding of agile psychology to practice agile leadership effectively.

AGILE INDUSTRY

The agility of businesses is limitless. When a company adopts an agile digital approach, it can have a widespread impact on its partners due to the interconnectedness and interdependence of many businesses in the digital landscape. Even government agencies responsible for audit and compliance may undergo a transformation. Leaders who embrace agility plan and strategize for industry-wide agility, acknowledging that organizational boundaries are fluid and permeable in the digital realm.

CONSOLIDATION WORKSHOP

1. In what ways can a leader utilize an Agile mind-map? If you were leading a team, which particular areas of the agile mind-map would you prioritize first? Please provide examples based on the Agile mind-map presented in this chapter.
2. What potential obstacles may an agile leader encounter if they have not understood the Agile mind-map? In other words, how important is it to know what comprises Agile?

3. How can cognitive, behavioral, and psychoanalytical aspects be incorporated into the practical application of Agility? Consider how you will develop an Agile transformation strategy based on these aspects.
4. What is the significance of the Agile Manifesto? Please discuss one statement of the manifesto you agree with and another you disagree with. Provide examples to support your argument.
5. What is the significance of the agile values? Why is it essential to comprehensively understand these values from a psycho-social standpoint to apply them in practice? What will happen if an organization applies Agile practices without giving due credence to the values?
6. Please discuss one agile principle from each of the four contextual groups of agile principles. Discuss the practical challenges of each principal. How does your psychological insight assist in implementing these agile principles in practice?
7. How can Agile practices (techniques) be utilized in a project? Please develop an approach to apply some practices from the list in job aids.
8. What is method friction? How can Agility reduce the effect of method friction?
9. Why is a composite approach to agile necessary, and what are its benefits and drawbacks? Please argue your case.

Chapter 3

Psychological frameworks and agile

CHAPTER SUMMARY

This chapter overviews popular psychological frameworks essential for understanding and implementing Agile psychology. The focus is on the memory mechanism, which is at the heart of these frameworks. We discuss how early childhood recordings influence personality formation and contribute to developing biases, which can pose challenges in an Agile environment. We also explore the concept of mindfulness and its potential to promote peaceful, enjoyable, and productive work. Not all frameworks discussed here are relevant in every situation, and individual preferences and personalities can influence their applicability. Overall, this chapter offers a comprehensive look at the available psychology frameworks essential for achieving Agile success.

INTRODUCTION

Agile practices and psychological frameworks overlap significantly, making them very interesting to agile leaders. The success of agility depends on insights from established disciplines like psychology and sociology. However, each psychological framework has its limitations and effectiveness. How leaders and team members interpret and understand these frameworks can unlock agile potential in the workplace. Agility promotes collaboration, communication, collective ownership, and self-management, which reduce stress, enhance output quality, and align outputs with organizational direction. However, agility's subjective and fuzzy nature, with a high value on individuals, presents a challenge. As Koch[1] says, "Experts fail to account for the infinite complexity that stems from each individual's unique needs

1 Koch, C., 2020, "People Aren't Problems," *Believe in People*, St. Martin Press, New York, p. 130 (Chapter 6).

DOI: 10.1201/9781003201540-3

and talents." Understanding each individual's unique needs and motivations makes it possible to implement agile in practice effectively.

Individual personalities, biases, personal goals, and motivations play a significant role in shaping an agile work environment. A person's behavior and how they are treated can significantly impact team dynamics, which in turn influences the overall organizational personality. Almost all adult behaviors are rooted in memory mechanisms developed from infancy. Therefore, a successful leader in an agile environment must learn these mechanisms and develop a deep understanding of the psychology of agile.

For example, a leader who understands the psychological nuances of agile can distinguish between introversion and extroversion, recognize the impact of biases, and understand the formation of gestalt in the work environment. Additionally, they will examine how a person's psychological makeup affects communication, collaboration, and decision-making. A good leader models mindfulness and continually promotes agile values.

Skilled leaders who incorporate psychological, sociological, and cultural principles in their work can smoothly transition their workplaces to agile workplaces. By tapping into the knowledge and expertise of those in fields beyond traditional project management, these leaders generate and apply valuable insights on how to guide individuals, teams, and organizations toward achieving agility.

An effective Agile leader understands that success cannot be achieved solely through rigid calculations of time, budget, and resources. Instead, they prioritize the complexities of human behavior and the impact of soft factors within the workplace when guiding their teams. Unfortunately, many workplaces prioritize professional and corporate growth over social consciousness, resulting in an over-reliance on analytical thinking skills, detailed standards, and precise metrics. However, these measurable parameters alone do not guarantee successful outcomes. There are numerous examples where projects appeared on track according to the iron triangle of time, budget, and resources and still the projects failed. Agile leadership acknowledges the delicate nature of human behavior, embraces contradictions, and understands the necessity of balancing technical, methodological, and social skills to achieve success in the digital world.

PSYCHOLOGICAL FRAMEWORKS

Familiarity with psychological and social frameworks can prove invaluable for professionals in these fields. It's especially useful to review and apply these frameworks when working within an agile work environment. Table 3.1 outlines some of the most widely recognized frameworks and highlights their potential to contribute to Agile's success.

Table 3.1 Psychosocial Frameworks and Their Potential Roles in Agile Success

Psycho-Social Frameworks	*Potential Role in Agile Success*
Freud's Psychoanalysis	Team members can use the psychoanalytic framework of id, ego, and super-ego to understand themselves better. However, applying this framework in IT and business work environments can be challenging due to its clinical complexity. It requires education and training to work as a psychoanalyst, which is not the primary expertise of an agile leader.
Jung's Gestalt	Team members are encouraged to approach projects holistically, understanding the gestalt of the project even if it cannot be easily measured. This framework prioritizes synthesis over analysis in a given work situation.
Maslow's Needs Hierarchy	Individual growth within teams and organizations can be charted using the needs hierarchy framework, which can be mapped to Agile work environments.
Berne's Transactional Analysis	Facilitating teamwork in Agile teams and organizations can be achieved by understanding TA's parent-adult-child roles, adopting the "I am OK;You are OK" life position, and avoiding gamy behavior. These are simple yet highly effective ways to incorporate agility in work.
Edward Bono's Six Thinking Hats	An agile work environment thrives on collaboration. The six thinking hats technique can be extremely useful to help an agile team discuss and focus on a common topic. This technique involves metaphorical hats that can direct the thought energies of the team in different meetings as per the topic being discussed.
Skinner's Conditioning Behavior	Provides a philosophical basis for the Agile work environment based on acceptance of change.
Hall's High-/Low-Context Cultures	Understanding the socio-cultural contexts of project teams across geographically dispersed boundaries is important in Agile projects. The high and low context cultures provide an excellent basis to adapt to the nuances of cross-cultural teams typical in an outsourced, off-shored agile project.
Hofstede's Culture	Provides a basic understanding of the cultural differences in communications and negotiations, particularly in outsourced and off-shore project work.
Gardner's Intelligences	Recognizing the various types of intelligence within an agile workplace creates opportunities for team members to learn, collaborate, and contribute in multiple ways. Individuals who excel in areas such as words, numbers, pictures, and music can be recognized for their strengths and allowed to express themselves.

Table 3.1 (Cont.)

Psycho-Social Frameworks	*Potential Role in Agile Success*
Sperry's Left-/Right-Brain Theories	The left-right brain theory provides a framework for integrating planned and Agile methodologies in a balanced manner. This balance is essential for agile leaders to guide transformation toward a composite agile work environment.
Kahneman's Fast and Slow Thinking	The human mind consists of two primary systems: the fast, intuitive, and emotional system and the slow, more deliberate, and logical system. Each individual possesses both of these systems and understanding their workings can help us recognize and address biases that may influence our decision-making.
Myers–Briggs' Type Indicator (MBTI)	Identifying MBTI and matching their personalities among Agile team members provides an opportunity to create a collaborative, self-organized team. Such a team reduces friction and promotes a smoother work environment.
Theory of Biases	Gain a better understanding of effective decision-making by examining and reducing biases that impact work.
Kabat-Zinn's Mindfulness	Mindfulness promotes awareness of decisions and actions, which highly benefits Agile teams that value trust, honesty, and unhurriedness.

PSYCHO-SOCIAL FRAMEWORKS AND AGILE LEADERSHIP

The psychological frameworks outlined in Table 3.1 are further explored in this section. The more detailed discussion that follows will be relevant depending leadership preferences and comfort level. A practical Agile workplace doesn't require the use of all the frameworks listed. Furthermore, each framework has unique nuances and suitability for certain leadership styles and personalities. The next two chapters will explore specific frameworks, such as transactional analysis (TA), Maslow, left-right brains, and slow-fast thinking, focusing on the Composite Agile Method and Strategy (CAMS).

Freud's psychoanalysis and agile

When it comes to understanding the workings of the mind, psychoanalysis, also known as the Freudian approach, is highly analytical. For an agile leader, a basic understanding of psychoanalysis can be a valuable tool. An agile leader is not expected to be a psychoanalyst. However, grasping concepts such as the id, ego, and super-ego benefits an agile work environment where individuals and their interactions are highly prioritized. By recognizing the deep-seated beliefs and emotions that influence behavior, leaders can better understand their team members and foster a more productive work environment. While detailed psychoanalysis reveals complex patterns and causes of behavior, simply appreciating the basics of Freud's analysis can provide some valuable insights for agile leaders without needing a formal process or tool. Additionally, psychological maturity is crucial for accepting change in an agile environment, as it can bring up anxieties for many individuals. Leaders need to anticipate and address these anxieties. Some psychological tools and frameworks discussed in this chapter are built upon Freudian theories. Hence, acquainting with psychoanalysis can help leaders apply suitable psychosocial frameworks more effectively.

Jung's gestalt and agile

Jung is well known for developing the concept of gestalt and classifying individuals based on archetypes. The gestalt concept is based on the subjective nature of mental perceptions. The same situation is likely to be viewed differently depending on the individual. Furthermore, the mind is inherently geared toward perceiving stimuli in a way that appears complete or whole. Philosophically, gestalt is different from analysis, which deals with understanding the individual parts of a stimulus. Gestalt moves towards a holistic view of a situation. For example, even if a sentence is slightly incomplete or inaccurate, the mind attempts to complete it: "Tihs is a cmopelte snetecne" is read by the mind as a complete sentence. This perception by the mind is not necessarily the reality, and gestalt may give the impression that a requirement is complete when it is not.

Gestalt can also be applied in contemporary technologies, such as Generative AI, to complete requirements and undertake Root Cause Analysis. In Agile projects, where documentation is light, tools are sparse, and contracts are not a priority, the mental ability to strive for completeness and symmetry (Wabi-Sabi) is immensely helpful. Gestalt plays a key part in the collaborative and communicative work environment in an Agile environment, requiring closer attention and awareness. The individuals' gestalt helps them perceive requirements, development, and testing in a holistic way, making gestalt in Agile the process of synthesis, rather than analysis.

Maslow's needs hierarchy and agile

Maslow's hierarchy of needs is a series of needs that individuals must meet incrementally to reach their full potential. In Chapter 5, this hierarchy is discussed in detail, along with brain theories and how it overlaps with Agile methods. An agile leader who understands this hierarchy can create a growth pathway for each team member. For instance, the leader can start by providing a workspace that meets the basic physiological requirements and is safe and supportive of the individual. The collaborative and non-competitive agile work environment encourages team members to apply the principles of self-motivation and self-organization, leading to constant improvement and growth. Eventually, this leads to Maslow's concept of self-actualization. Agile leaders who comprehend the hierarchy of needs are well placed to encourage team members to move toward self-actualization in a non-competitive work environment.

Berne's transactional analysis (TA) and agile

Berne's TA and Agile methodologies have a fascinating correlation that is likely to impact agile work areas significantly. TA argues that individuals have three ego states (Parent, Adult, and Child) that influence their behavior and interactions with others. Agile is an iterative and collaborative approach that is built on effective interactions between team members. Understanding the diverse ego states and leveraging a winning life position, team members can communicate more effectively and operate more efficiently. Agile environments prioritize transparency and authenticity, which aligns with Berne's notion of authenticity of communication. Moreover, Agile fosters a sense of individual responsibility and accountability for the team's success, consistent with Berne's adult ego state concept. Further exploration of this framework can be found in Chapter 4.

Edward de Bono's "six thinking hats" and agile

Edward de Bono's "Six Thinking Hats" is a valuable psychosocial framework that is helpful in directing the thought energies of an agile team in a specific direction. The collaborative nature of agile implies a need for guidance to capitalize on the thoughts and viewpoints of many individuals working together in a relatively informal work environment. Without guidance, individuals' thoughts and views will dissipate. Directing the thought processes by using colored hats helps consolidate group thinking. Each hat in this framework represents a particular style of thinking that the team is encouraged to explore. The Blue Hat represents planning and organization so that it can be helpful during agile iteration planning. The Green Hat encourages creative thinking, which the product owner can utilize to help the team develop unique analytical models and imaginative interfaces. The Red Hat directs the team to focus on their emotions and feelings, resulting in an excellent "retrospective" session at the end of an agile iteration. The Yellow Hat thinking focuses on the initiative's benefits, requiring the use of tools and data from the planned processes, such as time and budget. The Black Hat directs risk assessment and management, which is at the heart of agile success. The short, sharp iterations and sprints that showcase the product release while it is being developed is an excellent risk reduction mechanism. The White Hat deals with capturing information that can range from writing user stories and operational requirements to cybersecurity and relevant predictive models.

The yellow (harmony) and green (creativity) thinking hats are further relevant to an agile work environment. Creativity in an agile work environment results from harmony without negative competition. For example, when a group is protected from the outside and is encouraged to be creative without being task-managed, it becomes harmonious (Yellow Hat), and the working style and performance of such a group start generating nuggets of innovation that may not have been planned for (Green Hat). Making provisions for completely unexpected outputs and interweaving them with the general business direction is a vital Agile leadership characteristic that is very well supported by the "thinking hats."

Skinner's conditioning behavior

According to B.F. Skinner's conditioning theory states that behavior is influenced by external stimuli and reinforcement rather than individual free will and decision-making. In Agile methodology, this presents an opportunity to prioritize positive reinforcement. Punishment is often deemed ineffective in an Agile environment, so leaders focus on supporting, appreciating, and promoting excellence in collaboration and performance among team members. By continuously adjusting and improving their behavior based on feedback from the team and stakeholders during each iteration of work, individuals can enhance their performance and contribute to the team's success. The agile approach prioritizes collaboration and teamwork, which can serve as an external reinforcement. Team members can encourage and positively reinforce each other's behavior to achieve greater outcomes.

Hall's high-/low-context cultures and agile[2]

The effectiveness of a workplace hinges on the context in which work is conducted. Especially when implementing Agile methodologies, it is critical to consider the diverse cultural backgrounds and disparities among team members, as these factors offer valuable insights into their motivations and behaviors. According to Hall's theory, certain cultures place a heavy emphasis on shared context and implicit communication (high context), while others prioritize explicit communication and individualism (low context). High-context cultures facilitate communication and collaboration in an Agile working environment, with face-to-face interaction and cross-functional, co-located teams being common among team members from such backgrounds. Conversely, low-context cultures favor detailed, documentation-oriented approaches to planning and execution,

2 Hall, E. T., 1976, *Beyond Culture*, Anchor Books, New York, NY.

with formality, contracts, and metrics taking precedence over mutual understanding and informal agreements. By recognizing and adapting to these differences in communication styles, Agile teams can work more efficiently and prevent misunderstandings that might arise from cultural disparities. This, in turn, can foster stronger collaboration and ultimately lead to better outcomes for the team.

Hofstede's culture and agile

Hofstede's cultural dimensions theory[3] is a widely recognized framework that can offer significant insights into an Agile work environment. Specifically, the theory highlights the importance of comprehending cultural disparities when collaborating with teammates from diverse backgrounds. This is especially pertinent in off-shore, outsourced Agile work, where effective collaboration and teamwork across geographical regions are instrumental in delivering a successful solution. By considering cultural differences and customizing communication and collaboration strategies accordingly, Agile teams can work more efficiently and mitigate potential friction.

Gardner's multiple intelligences

Intelligence is a complex concept that goes beyond the conventional measures of Intelligence Quotient. In today's dynamic work environment, teams are made up of individuals with diverse backgrounds and skill sets. To ensure effective collaboration, it is essential to identify and utilize the various forms of intelligence that team members possess. According to Gardner,[4] there are eight distinct types of intelligence, each with its own implications for the workplace. While every team member has a range of intelligences, a skilled leader will prioritize the team's strongest areas of intelligence to promote a cohesive and productive team dynamic. below, keeping the agile workplace in mind:

- Linguistic intelligence refers to the ability to communicate effectively through language and create articulate descriptions of requirements in a project.
- Logical-mathematical intelligence is using numbers and reasoning to focus on budgeting, cost and time tracking, and prioritization.

3 *Geert Hofstede Site CV Work Life Theory 6 Dimensions of Culture Gert Jan, Geerthofstede.com* https://geerthofstede.com/culture-geert-hofstede-gert-jan-hofstede/6d-model-of-national-culture/ (Accessed: 18 July, 2024); Hofstede, G., *Dimensionalizing Cultures: The Hofstede Model in Context, ScholarWorks@GVSU. Online Readings in Psychology and Culture* (Accessed: 18 July, 2024); Hofstede, G., 1991, *Cultures and Organizations: Software of the Mind*, McGraw-Hill, London, ISBN 9780077074746.

4 Gardner, H., 1983, *Frames of Mind: The Theory of Multiple Intelligences*, Basic Books, New York, NY, USA.

- Spatial intelligence is related to the ability to create models, designs, architectures, and user interfaces in a typical software solutions project.
- Bodily-kinesthetic intelligence, also called "body smart," can recognize and interpret body language in a daily stand-up meeting or in a showcase exercise.
- Musical intelligence, or "music smart," can derive insights from tones of voices in an agile work environment.
- Interpersonal intelligence, also known as "people smart," utilizes theories of team formations to put together highly collaborative teams.
- Intrapersonal intelligence, or "self-smart," is the ability to implement agile principles of self-organization and self-direction easily.

Gardner later proposed existential and moral intelligences. Existential intelligence involves contemplating fundamental questions regarding our existence, such as who we are and why we exist. In an agile workplace, it is essential to encourage existential intelligence as it creates an environment that fosters relationships between team members that are not solely based on utility and goals. Existential intelligence allows more creativity and imagination to flourish within the agile teams. Moral intelligence may not play a direct role in the workplace but may still be present in the background.

Left-/right-brain theory and agile

The concept of left-brain/right-brain thinking, as defined by Sperry,[5] has important implications for Agile approaches. According to Sperry, the left side of the brain is responsible for analytical thinking, while the right is responsible for creative and intuitive thinking. As a result, left-brain thinking tends to be more verbose, document-centric, planning-heavy, and contract-driven. In contrast, right-brain thinking is more Agile, relying on face-to-face communications, shared ownership, trust, and visibility. To fully leverage Agile's benefits, a more holistic approach that engages both sides of the brain is required. This is known as composite Agile and is discussed in greater detail in Chapter 5. By integrating analytical and creative thinking, organizations can achieve greater flexibility, innovation, and adaptability in their Agile practices.

Kahneman's "fast and slow" thinking and agile

The relationship between Kahneman's fast and slow thinking and Agile methodologies is crucial in practicing the psychology of agile. In Agile work environments, a balance between quick, intuitive judgments and meticulous, methodical analysis is essential. Fast thinking is automatic and instinctive,

5 Sperry, R. "Some Effects of Disconnecting the Cerebral Hemispheres," *Science*, 217(4566), 1223–1226.

while slow thinking involves careful contemplation and analysis. However, fast thinking may lead to potential biases, while measured, slow thinking encourages a strong foundation for comprehensive, strategic thinking. Being aware and mindful of both types of thinking in mind can assist Agile teams in making better-informed and more efficient decisions.

Myers–Briggs' personality indicators (MBTI) and agile

Briggs and Myers created the MBTI[6] to simplify personality classification. It consists of four personality traits, extending Jung's work mentioned earlier.

E (extroversion) or I (introversion)
S (sensing) or N (intuition)
T (thinking) or F (feeling)
J (judging) or P (perceiving)

One letter from each of the pairs results in a four-character personality type. For example, an ESTJ personality type is an extrovert who is sensing, thinking, and judging.

Integrating Myers–Briggs' personality test indicators (MBTI) in agile teams can significantly enhance their effectiveness. By comprehending the personality types of team members, Agile teams can optimize their strengths and work together more efficiently. For instance, an introverted team member may prefer independent work on certain tasks, while a more extroverted team member may thrive in a collaborative setting.

E individuals are outgoing, whereas the I personalities prefer to look inward. The strengths of the E personalities, such as being talkative, outgoing, and conversation initiators, can be used by astute project leaders to place these individuals in contact with business stakeholders, users, and domain experts. On the other hand, introverts or I personalities (who are relatively quiet and reserved) perform better, for example, in dealing with enterprise and business architects. This is because architectural work requires less people interactions than business analysis work, and it benefits from sitting down and modeling from a stable rather than a changing viewpoint. Thus, understanding these personality traits can also lead to appropriate recruitment and resource management suitable for Agile organizational culture. This understanding can also enable the successful uplifting of well-aligned internal capabilities within and across groups.

Leaders can benefit from understanding their personality type, as it can help them determine whether they tend to be authoritative or whether they are likely to give their team members more freedom to work independently.

6 Briggs, K. C., 1987, *Myers-Briggs Type Indicator. Form G*, Consulting Psychologists Press, Palo Alto, CA, USA.

The MBTI can also be used to describe the personality of a team as a whole. For instance, a team may display characteristics of an ISTJ personality type on some occasions, while at other time it may exhibit traits of an ENFP personality type. MBTI and other frameworks like TA and Six Thinking Hats of de Bono are extremely useful in Agile transformations.

MBTI personality types are not absolute and should not be treated as fixed characteristics. MBTI is an indicative framework and not a predictive tool for psychosocial behavior. Depending on the circumstances, individuals may exhibit traits that differ from their assigned personality type.

Theory of biases and agile

When implementing Agile methods, it's important to consider the potential impact of biases. By acknowledging and addressing personal biases and those of team members, informed decisions can be made, leading to a more efficient Agile process. Understanding theories related to biases, such as slow-fast thinking, can help better grasp the concept. Recognizing that the fast-thinking brain may be susceptible to bias is an effective tool in mitigating its effects. Additionally, knowing the Myers–Briggs' personality indicators can promote greater understanding and empathy among team members. Agile leaders who remain vigilant for biases in their observations, data, analytics, and decision-making can foster a collaborative work environment that encourages productivity and happiness.

Kabat-Zinn's mindfulness and agile

Mindfulness, developed by Kabat-Zinn,[7] is a self-care approach that enables individuals to manage stress. It is a valuable tool in Agile work environments, where it can effectively enhance focus, reduce stress, and encourage teamwork. Mindfulness techniques like meditation and deep breathing are particularly helpful for Agile teams. By promoting relaxed focus, collaborative decision-making and problem-solving, fostering improved communication and collaboration, and reducing burnout, mindfulness creates opportunities for Agile teams to establish a culture of well-being. Practicing continuous improvement and retrospectives, emphasizing mindful leadership and team-building, and promoting mindful communication and active listening are all ways Agile teams can achieve this culture of well-being.

MEMORY MECHANISMS AND THE AGILE MANIFESTO

The various psychological frameworks that are used to understand human behavior and thought processes originate from an individual's mind. The mind, in turn, is shaped by the memory imprints recorded in the brain.

7 Kabat-Zinn, J., 2005, *Wherever You Go There You Are* (10th ed.), Hyperion, New York, NY.

Therefore, it is important to understand the recording mechanisms and the interplay between the brain and the mind. A skilled Agile coach is aware of their memory mechanism, which enables them to comprehend and apply the psychological frameworks discussed earlier.

Brain mind mechanism

The brain is the intricate hardware that facilitates the transmission of countless messages between neurons, enabling an array of mental functions. Meanwhile, the mind can be regarded as the software that operates within the brain. The formation of neural pathways in the brain creates thoughts. Since a significant amount of thinking is a product of neurons that were activated during childhood, thinking is heavily influenced by early childhood memories. Although education and experience can alter the content of thoughts, the foundational parameters of thinking established in childhood can potentially restrict the length and breadth of cognition.

The Agile work environment is known for promoting individual freedom, which can lead to a range of subjective thoughts and opinions. However, this can also result in perceptions and biases that need to be taken into account. It's important to recognize how memory mechanisms impact individual viewpoints and biases, as this can greatly impact the success of Agile projects.

The external reality is far more than just an organized set of data points. In fact, it is a constantly evolving and complex entity, as depicted in Figure 3.1, that is difficult to define. Our minds are constantly at work,

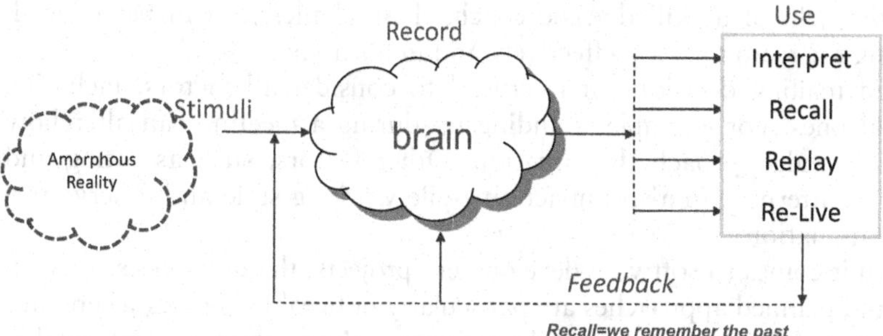

Figure 3.1 Brain Functions – Recording, Interpretation, Recall, Replay and Relive.

sifting through this intricate reality, separating the extraneous details and breaking down the vast and complicated components into more manageable pieces. Ultimately, we are able to synthesize these relevant pieces together to form a more comprehensive understanding of the world.

The memory mechanism involves various stages from stimuli to recording and usage. The brain acts as a digital recorder, imprinting and storing every experience from birth. Penfield's experiments provide essential insight into memory recording and recall.[8] Figure 3.1 summarizes this process, which includes interpretation, recall, replay, and reliving. Childhood experiences deeply ingrained in the brain's recorder can trigger distorted perceptions and reactions in current situations, impacting communication and collaboration in Agile projects. Team members can improve communication skills and build trust by understanding how brain recordings work. By being mindful of our mental processes, we can work together to create positive organizational change. For example, individuals aware of their memory records and replays can avoid involuntary reactions that lead to misunderstanding or conflict.

The success of an Agile team hinges on careful cultivation of the work culture, as the fabric of such a group can be quite delicate. An Agile coach who understands the way in which the brain replays and relives memories can handle potentially harmful stimuli that might otherwise damage the team's cohesion. For instance, if a user needs to change requirements, it's important to convey this information to the developer in a way and at a time that won't trigger negative memories. Past experiences with similar changes from authority figures like teachers or parents can lead to *reliving* of those experiences even if the individual isn't consciously able to remember them. With the help of a skilled Agile coach, these challenges can be reduced, allowing the team to work effectively and in harmony.

When making decisions, it is crucial to consider all factors, including physical ones. For example, standing up during a meeting can alter how we think and approach the situation. Other factors, such as eating and sleeping patterns, can also impact an Agile working style and deserve further examination.

When it comes to software development projects, the differences between Agile and planned approaches are particularly noticeable in cases where outsourcing or offshoring is involved. This is because the flexibility and informality of Agile can be at odds with the need for more formal planning, contracts, and service-level agreements. As illustrated in Figure 3.2, this dichotomy is emphasized by focusing on the right side of the manifesto. While individuals

8 Penfield, W., 1957, "Thoughts on the Function of the Temporal Cortex," *Neurosurgery*, 4(Supplement 1), pp. 21–33. https://doi.org/10.1093/neurosurgery/4.cn_suppl_1.21; and Penfield, W., 2008, "The Rôle of the Temporal Cortex in Recall of Past Experience and Interpretation of the Present," *Novartis Foundation Symposia*, John Wiley & Sons, Ltd, Chichester, UK, pp. 149–174.

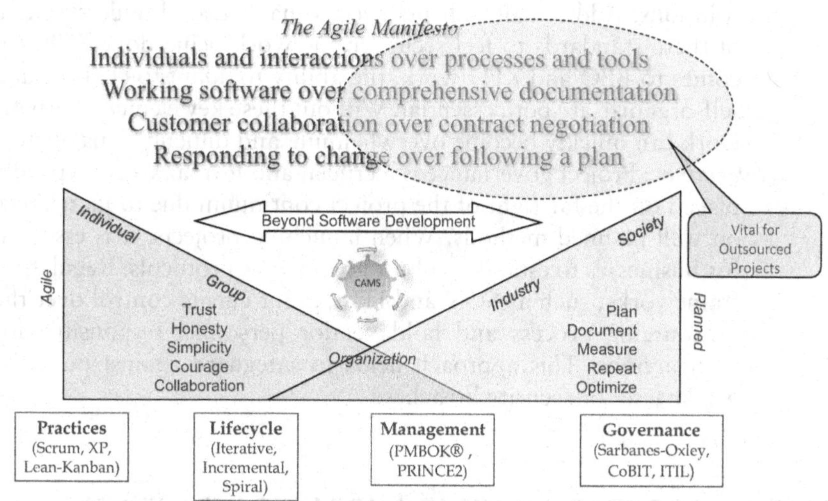

Figure 3.2 Psychological Disciplines, the Agile Manifesto, and the Balancing Act between Agile and Planned Values.

may be able to adopt Agile practices in IT projects that involve outsourcing, implementing them across groups or organizations can be challenging due to the greater levels of process rigor and governance required in industrial and social contexts beyond what Agile can provide. As shown in Figure 3.2, CAMS combines lifecycles, management, and governance to minimize friction between these frameworks. A CAMS-based Agile work environment would need to consider four key components, which are briefly outlined here.

Practices: Adopting Agile practices based on Agile methods like Scrum and XP is crucial for software development. These practices enable vendors to fully leverage their potential in the solution space and collaborate with clients to achieve superior results. Hence, these practices are predominantly derived from Agile methods and are depicted closer to the Agile approach in Figure 3.2.

Lifecycle: The approach to creating a solution using the lifecycle is decided through a collaborative effort between agile leaders, the client, and business stakeholders. Regarding outsourced solutions development, the project vendor may advocate for agility in the lifecycle, whereas the client may prioritize thorough planning and documentation.

Management: Standards such as PMBOK or PRINCE2 can be incredibly useful in estimating costs, time, and scope, all critical components of managing and controlling a project. These aspects are closely aligned with the traditional Waterfall approach to developing solutions. Additionally, clients need to have a solid understanding of these standards to feel secure in the work being done. When it comes to BPO and KPO work, the ability to adapt to changes and self-organize are both essential. Without these key elements, project work can quickly become overwhelming and difficult to navigate.

Governance: Project governance is a crucial and formal aspect typically placed on the far right of the project continuum due to its reliance on well-planned methods. When launching projects, it is essential for businesses to establish robust governance protocols. Regulatory frameworks, such as SOX and ITIL, grant clients control over the outsourcing process and hold vendor personnel responsible for their actions. This approach helps to safeguard against potential weaknesses or security breaches.

BIASES IN DECISION-MAKING AND THEIR IMPACT ON AGILE

Ongoing decision-making

Effective leadership in an Agile environment demands continuous and prompt decision-making across all stages of a project. For instance, during a daily stand-up, the product owner may propose modifying a user story, and team members must promptly contemplate its implications. An Agile coach may consider multiple options while another team member highlights the challenges of incorporating a search function within the Scrum framework. When an organization adopts an Agile methodology, this decision-making process becomes pervasive, encompassing all aspects, from accounting and marketing to inventory and beyond. However, it's imperative for all team members to acknowledge the likelihood of their decision-making being influenced by biases and approach it with great caution and respect to ensure as much impartiality and fairness as is possible.

Stereotypes and decisions

Stereotypes are preconceived notions that individuals may hold about certain groups, and they have the potential to distort one's perceptions, resulting in the endorsement of pre-existing expectations about others.[9] When making decisions, people tend to be swayed more by the value of potential outcomes rather than the probabilities involved, which can lead to

9 Weiten, W., 2010, *Psychology Themes and Variations* (8th ed.), Cengage Learning, Wadsworth, CA, USA.

inaccuracies in judgment. It is crucial to acknowledge these biases and strive to overcome them to achieve the most informed and efficient decisions. The field of psychology offers insights into diverse viewpoints, which can assist us in scrutinizing our actions and identifying decision-making biases.

Biases and their impacts on decision-making

In a discussion by T.K. Das and B.S. Teng,[10] various biases in strategic decision-making are explored. These biases can restrict our viewpoint and lead us to close-minded thinking. They may arise from inadequate information, outside influences, or an excessive reliance on our own convictions. The four main types of biases are perception, estimation and belief, social and group, and memory. Perception biases happen when our emotions or preconceived notions impact what we perceive. For example, we may unfairly assess someone's credibility based on appearance or behavior. Estimation and belief biases occur when we are certain about something without all the facts, leading us to be overly confident or careless in our decision-making. Social and group biases stem from our inclination to conform to others' opinions or actions, even if they are incorrect. Memory biases occur when our recollections are altered by our emotions or beliefs, resulting in inaccurate memories or incomplete recollections. Recognizing these biases is crucial to making informed decisions and treating others with fairness.

Perception biases

Perception biases can strongly influence the way we perceive reality. These biases are often based on our preconceived values and ideas, which can cause us to interpret things in a distorted way. These biases can manifest in various forms, such as bias blind spots (where an individual is unaware of a risky situation), illusion of control (where a person feels in control of a situation that they may not be), and similarity heuristic (where one scenario is wrongly compared to another). Sometimes, our perception of our own role or position may differ from reality. To overcome these biases, it's important to separate the "I" as "thought or perceived by me" from the "real" I. One effective strategy is to engage in friendly and informal discussions with colleagues. In more serious cases, it may be helpful to seek professionals with expertise in identifying and addressing these biases. Achieving unbiased perception can be difficult, but it is essential for building a strong Agile culture within an organization. When organizations adopt Agile, it's crucial to understand these biases and work to mitigate their negative impact on group dynamics.

10 Das, T. K. and Teng, B.S. "Cognitive Biases and Strategic Decision Processes: An Integrative Perspective," *Journal of Management Studies*, 1999, 36(6), 757–778.

Estimation and belief biases

Estimating the amount of work required for Agile projects can present a considerable challenge as biases can come into play. These biases can stem from overconfidence, misplaced optimism, and an inability to make necessary adjustments, ultimately leading to inaccurate estimations. Consequently, team members may overestimate or underestimate the work needed for a task based on their beliefs and assumptions. Such biases have the potential to result in missed deadlines, reduced productivity, and even project failure.

Social and group biases

Social and group biases can greatly affect team dynamics and decision-making processes. Examples of such biases include favoritism toward specific team members, groupthink, and stereotyping based on roles within the team. These biases stem from collective assumptions and preconceptions, such as the false consensus, bandwagon, and polarization effects. It is imperative to acknowledge and address these biases while seeking external feedback to ensure the ultimate success of an Agile project.

Memory biases

The way we remember past events can be affected by memory biases, which can either help or hinder our ability to recall depending on the situation. This can greatly impact decision-making, particularly in group environments like Agile workstyles where differing opinions may arise. In order to tackle these biases, it's best to handle the issue with sensitivity and encourage open discussion among group members. However, it's crucial to avoid making the conversation personal and avoid calling out biases directly. Sometimes, it may be helpful to postpone the discussion for a later time or use humor to help individuals see things from others' perspectives. Effective leaders understand the importance of managing memory biases in a fair and positive manner to encourage positive group dynamics and decision-making.

INFLUENCE OF BIASES ON AGILE WORK ENVIRONMENTS

In an Agile environment, biases can have a significant impact on specific areas. To combat these biases, it is essential that Agile teams regularly review and adjust their estimates. Facilitating open communication and collaboration is crucial in identifying and addressing biases. By acknowledging and dealing with these biases, Agile teams can improve their accuracy and effectiveness in project delivery. However, biases can also affect methods like Delphi and MoSCoW, leading to incorrect numbers and team tension. To prevent such issues, teams must prioritize consensus-building over relying solely on numbers or voting. Moreover, cross-checking with past project data and seeking input from external parties can help mitigate the impact of biases. Teams that are aware of these biases and work toward reducing their influence can foster a more inclusive and effective work environment, leading to successful project outcomes. Following are some suggestions for mitigating the impact of biases in agile work.

1. *Project management:* In Agile environments, it's crucial to remember that the project management process is informal. This entails that daily estimations of work and priorities are determined through collaboration and discussions. However, estimation and belief biases can significantly hinder Agile project management. To overcome these biases, one can compare estimates with past estimates of similar projects, seek expert guidance, and apply parameters to make estimates.
2. *Business analysis:* Gathering functional and non-functional requirements is crucial in business analysis. While Agile methodologies often employ user stories to document these requirements, other techniques like use cases, activity graphs, and Business Process Modeling Notations (BPMNs) are also commonly used. One major obstacle in business analysis is the presence of social and group biases, which can make group workshops, interviews, and discussions particularly challenging. To combat these biases, it is essential to approach business analysis with an open and impartial mindset that considers all perspectives. Tools such as fishbone diagrams and asking "why" five times can aid in identifying the root causes of issues and gathering comprehensive requirements without bias.
3. *Architecture and development:* Agile projects involve constantly integrating architecture and development work areas. However, personal biases may inadvertently impact assumptions and constraints for a proposed solution. Composite Agile seeks to counteract this by merging the stability of architecture with the iterative and incremental nature of agile development, thus minimizing the impact of personal biases and vested interests.
4. *Quality assurance and testing:* Agile development places great emphasis on integrating quality assurance and testing with the overall development process and architecture. However, it's crucial to acknowledge that quality assurance and testing necessitate a dedicated and distinct effort, as subjective factors can significantly impact their efficacy. The perception of quality can greatly influence testing efforts. By maintaining an unwavering commitment to quality and implementing rigorous testing procedures, Agile can guarantee that its products meet the most rigorous performance and reliability standards.
5. *Cybersecurity:* The realm of cybersecurity is intricate and encompasses multiple components, including technologies, procedures, and

individuals. It's essential to bear in mind that biases can subjectively influence cybersecurity. Depending on the biases of those in charge, a project can be tightly or loosely secured. Cybersecurity demands careful consideration of factors such as encryption strength, cloud backup processes, and guiding users to cultivate sound security practices. Biases can obstruct cybersecurity efforts or leave an entry point vulnerable to cyberattacks. It's vital to approach cybersecurity with impartiality and equity to ensure optimal protection.

6. *Training:* Recognizing the impact of biases on training is crucial. Depending on various factors, such as social and group biases, it may be necessary to provide team members with significant training, mentoring, and coaching to enable them to perform effectively in an agile project. Moreover, training can help individuals overcome their biases, ultimately benefiting the project. However, if a leader's perception or social bias is present, training may not be effective. It is equally essential to consider biases when it comes to end-user training, as this can profoundly impact the project's success.

CONSOLIDATION WORKSHOP

1. Why is understanding psychological and social frameworks important when applying agile in practice? What can happen if the agile leader does not understand the underlying psychology of individuals and groups?
2. Which mental process involved in agility is emphasized by cognitive psychology? Which behavioral aspects of agility are focused on by behavioral psychology? How does psychoanalytical psychology examine the unconscious aspects of agility?
3. Can you explain how Jung's gestalt therapy is connected to the concept of synthesis versus analysis when applying Agile methodologies in real-world situations?
4. Please explain the five levels of Maslow's needs hierarchy and their direct correlation to Agile methodology.
5. What's the significance of having a theory of social interactions in Agile work environments, as Eric Berne suggests in transactional analysis?
6. What are some common cultural challenges that Agile teams may face when working across borders?
7. Can Agile principles be adapted to fit different cultural norms and values? If so, discuss with examples how you would apply some of the agile principles in an outsourced, off-shored project with team members from different cultural backgrounds?
8. What role does effective communication play in bridging cultural differences within an Agile team?

9. How can cross-cultural training help Agile teams navigate cultural differences and achieve better results?
10. In your opinion, which side of the brain is more dominant in Agile – left or right? Can you elaborate on why you think so?
11. How important is mindfulness in an Agile culture? Can you provide some examples of how it can impact team communications and morale?
12. What is the underlying basis of brain function? Can you explain how the analogy of a "tape recorder" helps in understanding brain function?
13. How does the perception of "I" affect communication? Can you give examples from your personal experience?
14. What are biases and how do they impact decision-making?
15. Out of the four biases discussed (perception, estimation and belief, social and group, and memory biases), which two do you think are the most challenging and how would you handle them as an agile leader?
16. Out of various project areas discussed (project management, business analysis, architecture and development, quality assurance and testing, and cybersecurity) consider any two with examples, in terms of how biases influence them and your approach to overcoming bias.

Chapter 4

Transactional analysis (TA) and agile leadership

CHAPTER SUMMARY

This chapter focuses on applying the transactional analysis (TA) framework in an Agile work environment. TA is a highly effective mechanism for social interactions that can provide psychological and social guidance to practitioners. The chapter explains TA's various components, such as ego states, transactions, life positions, and games, making it an easy-to-use framework for Agile leaders. This chapter explains the three ego states (Parent, Adult, and Child) and the corresponding four life positions, which are essential for practicing TA. Additionally, the chapter outlines practical ways to implement TA by promoting agile values such as trust and honesty. The wasteful game-playing activities are also highlighted, with examples from IT projects. Finally, the chapter maps the Myers–Briggs personality indicators to the TA ego states as a means to adopting Agile at work.

INTRODUCTION

People are the key to producing quality products and providing exceptional service. There is a certain level of "goodness," embodied by people working in teams which is not easily defined but can be tangibly felt. Tapping into that goodness and bringing it out is a leadership capability. Smooth and positive interactions between people provide a workplace with minimal friction and maximum goodness. TA is a simple yet highly effective tool for promoting positive social interactions within Agile workplaces. Agile leaders don't need to be experts in psychology, but possessing basic social interaction skills and techniques can help facilitate work in a joyful manner and promote value. Agile, which originated in software development, leans toward the artistic and right-brained human nature. A software product's value, whether a mobile app, cloud-based application, or Artificial Intelligence (AI)-assisted analytics, is subjective because it depends on the user's context and relevance, which changes far more rapidly than the users of physical goods. Leaders have long relied on works such as Demarco and Lister's

DOI: 10.1201/9781003201540-4

Peopleware[1] and Constantine and Meyer's emphasis on the importance of the "human factor."[2] In particular, Constantine says "Good software does not come from CASE tools, visual programming, rapid prototyping, or object technology. Good software comes from people. So does bad software." Even as we look toward the future of AI and digital advancements, people's role and subjectivity in decision-making cannot be underestimated. This subjectivity permeates the agile culture, necessitating awareness among leaders and team members of numerous elements of human motivations at work that cannot be objectively measured. The prioritization of a user story and the number of iterations are examples of agile ceremonies with subjectivity. Furthermore, the traditional "carrot and stick" approach of managers is absent in an agile work environment. Agile teams are "self-organized and self-managed," necessitating a deeper understanding of human nature and interactions than a formal, planned, Waterfall-based approach to work.

AWARENESS AND COMMUNICATION

Awareness is an integral part of working in an Agile environment. Awareness is also the key to practicing TA. This is so because awareness of one's action, arising out of one's personality, enables effective communication and collaboration. When a cross-functional, cross-cultural agile team is put together, wide variations in cultural nuances, motivations, biases, and social skills are expected. These variations play a vital role in the daily activities of Agile projects. Leaders need a simple yet effective mechanism to span the cultural width and handle individual biases in an environment that is not planned and hierarchical. Agile leaders and team members need psychological mechanisms that can enhance their social and cognitive skills and reduce friction at work.

TA is a streamlined and impactful approach to practical psychology that agile teams can use without a psychologist's expertise. Furthermore, the principles outlined in TA align harmoniously with the Agile Manifesto and values, making it a valuable tool for Agile leaders to enable a shared vision and acceptance of individual accountability. TA provides all the necessary elements to help leaders handle soft factors based on personality traits in the workplace. Popularized by authors like Berne (1964)[3] and Harris (1973),[4]

1 DeMarco, T., and Lister, T., 1987, *Peopleware: Productive Projects and Team*, Dorset House, New York, NY.

2 Constantine, L., 1995, *Constantine on Peopleware*, Yourdon Press, Upper Saddle River, NJ; Constantine, L., Panel on "Soft Issues and Other Hard Problems in Software Development," *OOPSLA'96*, San Jose, CA, USA, October 1996.

3 Berne, E., 1964, *Games People Play*, Penguin, New York, NY.

4 Harris, T. A. (1969). *I'm OK, you're OK*, Harper & Row, New York, NY.

TA has been widely applied in management through works like *The OK Boss*[5] and *Practical TA in Management.*[6]

Understanding the impact of individual personality traits on communication and collaboration can help team members increase efficiency, reduce conflicts, and minimize stress. Recognizing the diverse personalities in the workplace can assist in managing intangible factors that are often difficult to quantify. Integrating TA with Agile practices improves communication, increases self-awareness, and strengthens team relationships. However, potential challenges associated with implementing TA in Agile leadership, such as engaging in "game playing," should be considered. Self-awareness is important for leaders who want to incorporate TA into an agile workplace. TA is a valuable tool for identifying and categorizing various personalities in an agile project including that of the leader. This is because TA is most helpful in recognizing team members' ego states and adjusting communication styles accordingly. By using TA, leaders can identify the psychological states that individuals may experience during communication, tailor their communication style, and minimize miscommunication, misunderstandings, and conflicts. Agile leaders understand and expect the idiosyncrasies of individuals on their teams. Awareness of the uniqueness of each individual promotes a positive work environment, better team collaboration, and productivity.

PERSONAS AND VIEWS

Understanding how TA can be practically applied in an agile work environment starts with examining individuals' perspectives and beliefs. Every person carries a unique self-concept, primarily shaped during childhood and influenced by various factors such as parental figures, teachers, friends, and media sources. TA suggests that this self-concept, or persona, is not the true essence of a person. Awareness of one's persona is a liberating factor from the constraints of persona-driven interactions.

Persona

The agile approach is highly dependent on collaboration, which relies heavily on how two or more individuals interact with each other. Personas within TA provides an excellent window to understanding the dynamics of team communication. Recognizing the different roles and behaviors that individuals may adopt in group settings provides an improved opportunity

5 James, M., 1975, *The OK Boss*, Addison-Wesley Publishing Company, Reading, MA; James, M., & Jongeward, D. (1975). *Transactional analysis for students*, Addison-Wesley Longman, Reading, MA.

6 Morrison, J. H., and O'Hearne, J. J., 1977, *Practical Transactional Analysis in Management*, Addison-Wesley Educational, Reading, MA.

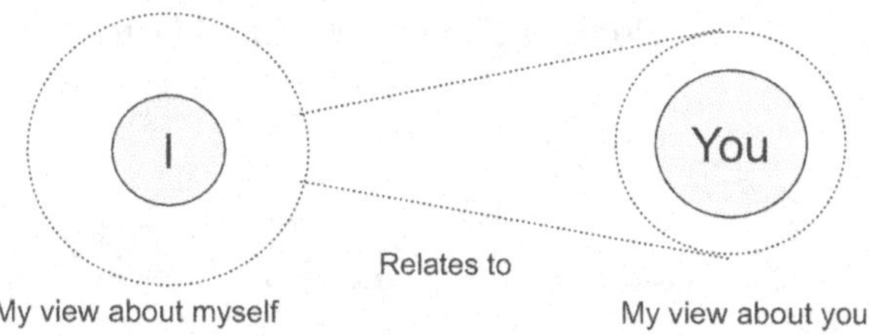

Figure 4.1 Collaboration Depends Heavily on Personas, Which Are Based on "Views" rather than Reality.

to navigate conflicts and build stronger relationships. In the context of the Agile approach, applying this theory can lead to more productive and harmonious team interactions, ultimately resulting in better project outcomes.

The theory of personas is based on the concept that the "I" we perceive ourselves to be is not necessarily the true version of ourselves, but rather the version we believe ourselves to be. This perception, shown in Figure 4.1, is what forms our persona. When engaging with others in a group setting such as an Agile team, the interaction of the "I" is with the persona we have created of that individual, rather than the person themselves. It's important to recognize that when we interact with others, we may not be interacting with the real person in front of us. We are interacting with our view of ourselves, their view of themselves, and their view of us, which can be influenced by a variety of sociocultural factors. This can lead to confusion and chaos, as the two individuals may have vastly different perceptions of one another.

Agile leaders develop this crucial understanding of how individuals and groups interact and take steps to bridge the gaps in understanding. Figure 4.2, based on "Johari's Window," depicts the nuances of a persona: what the person thinks of herself, what the person thinks others think of her, and what she really is. Personas can be labeled for improved understanding once individuals become aware of the differences between them and their existential reality. In an agile environment, leaders can facilitate the creation of individual personas or avatars for each team member that represent their specific responsibilities for various aspects of the project. These avatars can be made into small sticky labels and placed on user stories on a wall or board, which allows everyone to quickly and easily identify who is responsible for what. Separating the personas from the actual individuals is a neat agile technique that forms the basis for collective responsibility and smooth teamwork. By taking the time to create these personas, team members can gain a better

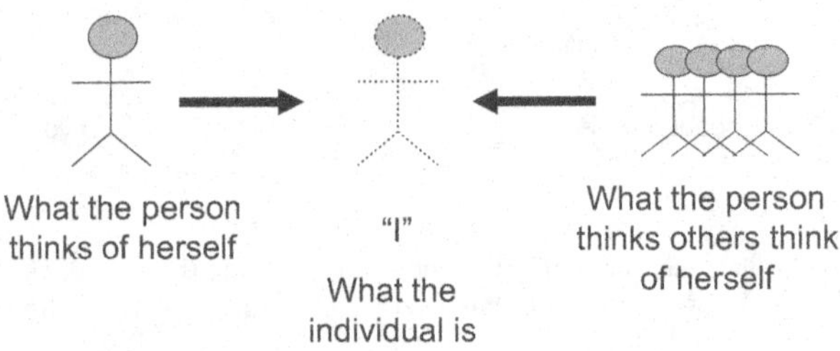

Figure 4.2 Individual's Views (Based on Johari's Window).

understanding of each other's unique skill sets and responsibilities, which can lead to streamlined collaboration and improved project results.

Transactional analysis (TA) basics

TA has long been a cornerstone of management studies due to its practicality and ease of comprehension.[7] The theory underlying TA is rooted in the memory mechanism, as explained in Chapter 3. It serves as a framework for understanding how childhood experiences shape a person's psyche. These experiences are stored and replayed in everyday interactions, ultimately impacting one's professional life. TA essentially comprises ego states, life positions, and games. There are three ego states: Parent, Adult and Child. Life position is a person's worldview, which forms in early childhood and persists throughout life regardless of changes in circumstances and emotions. The life position guides an individual's behavior, and even groups like teams, organizations, and nations possess "personality traits" based on their respective life positions.[8] TA offers a behavioral framework for comprehending how the memory mechanism influences our actions and how that behavior can be positively modified.

EGO STATES, TRANSACTIONS, AND AGILE

Each person has different ego states that drive their interactions with others. These states are formed during early childhood experiences and are

7 James, M., and Jongeward, D., 1975, *People Book: Transactional Analysis for Students*, Addison Wesley Longman Publishing, Reading, MA.

8 Harris, T. A., 1969, *I'm OK, You're OK: A Practical Guide to Transactional Analysis*, Harper & Row, New York.

considered "phenomenological realities" that exist within a person. Ego states are not the same as actual parents, adults, and children; therefore, they are capitalized in TA. The three ego states are as follows:

1. *"Parent" (controlling, protecting):* The Parent essentially comprises the taught concept of life. This information is recorded from parental sources and is dated or archaic. In the case of the Parent, the ego is the *rules enforcer and judge of what is right and wrong.*
2. *"Child" (emotional):* The Child is the felt concept of life. This is the emotional part of a person. The Child ego state within a person, irrespective of the biological age, is the *fun or tears expresser without concern for the protocols.*
3. *"Adult" (factual):* The Adult is the thought concept of life. The logical part of the mind figures out what is happening out there. The ego, in the case of an Adult, is the *reality tester that separates the rules and the emotions from the factual work.*

The ego states known as Parent and Child are formed through the memory mechanism previously discussed. Memories imprinted during early childhood, typically between the ages of six and eight, remain readily available for retrieval when subjected to a sensory input similar to the one that created the original impression in the mind. In contrast, the Adult ego state is based on observation of reality, free from the influence of parental factors or childlike emotions. Each of the three ego states is active in a person, and their effectiveness can be enhanced by developing awareness of their existence and impact. When used appropriately, each ego state can contribute positively and creatively to a person's life. Understanding the ego states is crucial for ensuring an agile team's smooth functioning and the organization's transition to agility and balance. Therefore, the following section delves deeper into the discussion of ego states in the context of an agile work environment.

Parent ego state

The Parent ego state is characterized by a strong sense of right and wrong, creating and enforcing rules, following protocols, offering guidance, and providing protection. Individuals with a strong Parent may find it challenging to work in an agile environment because of its informal and collaborative structure. The Parent state insists on following agile guidelines, such as the duration of a daily stand-up meeting or the format of a user story. This behavior is learned through past experiences with authority figures and controls actions in the Parent state. Awareness of this state can help reduce its overbearing influence at work. Conflict can arise from the Parent state of team members. However, the Parent state also benefits leaders in protecting their team from external influences because the original parent is always protective. This allows the team to focus on their work while the leader handles external issues.

Child ego state

The Child ego state represents the emotional concept of life and exhibits qualities similar to a child's, such as spontaneity, playfulness, and emotional reactions. Our childhood experiences and learned expressions can determine whether our Child ego state is creative and free or prone to rebellion and tantrums. It is crucial to be aware of our inner Child for agile teams to function smoothly, as agile principles of self-organization and self-direction can be properly applied only by understanding the Child ego state. While allowing the Child to express itself through fun and laughter is beneficial, its insecurity can create friction in agile teams and challenge the values of trust and honesty. Understanding and reflecting on emotional triggers similar to when the original Child was recorded is immensely helpful in the smoother functioning of agile teams. For example, the Child of many team members can get "hooked" during sprint Retrospectives where the "way we worked" is inspected by the team itself. Keeping the Child in check can greatly improve team performance. Additionally, the Child ego state is a vital source of humor and laughter in agile teams.

Adult ego state

The Adult ego state in TA pertains to life's rational and factual aspects. This is part of an individual's personality and enables decision-making based on reason and objectivity rather than emotions or past experiences. The Adult is an objective problem solver and an efficient decision-maker, making it a valuable asset for leaders of agile teams who encourage critical problem-solving and team members to develop objectivity. Compared to the Parent and Child ego states, the Adult is dimensionally different as it is an entity within us that is developed through education, training, and experience. It contains the agile techniques to be practiced and the tools for developing solutions, and it can even help sift the Parent and Child away from a conflicting situation. By promoting the use of the Adult among agile team members and leaders, an excellent work environment can be created that encourages all team members to work together toward the goals of the Sprint. Additionally, the Adult can anticipate and handle change, which is a crucial element of the agile working style. The Adult ego state develops and flourishes with a positive, OK atmosphere in which there is plenty of "stroking" from fellow team members and the facilitator.

Applying personas to transactions

Figure 4.3 concisely illustrates a persona that represents the "I." This "I" is composed of the three ego states previously discussed, which are phenomenological realities. Hence, these ego states are present in every individual. However, the persona also comprises an image of the "I," depicted on the right side of Figure 4.3. Understanding the "I" and the image of the "I" (as explained in Figure 4.2 with Johari's window) implies that an individual can have multiple personalities. In an agile work environment, this knowledge of multiple personalities is useful in explaining why a communicative person in the morning may suddenly become reserved and quiet later in the day. It is possible that the Adult part of their personality was in charge of transactions (behavior) in the morning, but as the day progressed, either the Parent or Child ego state took over. The taking over of either the Parent or the Child ego state is based on sensory inputs during the day which are not all related work or people. For example, a team member's Child can get "hooked" if the weather is too hot or cold and the AC is not working; a Parent can get "hooked" by a team member fiddling with their notes or dress. As awareness of these ego states grows, team members gain more freedom to initiate or respond from any of the three states, creating opportunities for collaborative work, understanding cross-cultural differences, and minimizing friction in the workplace. The following section will discuss how personas interact through transactions.

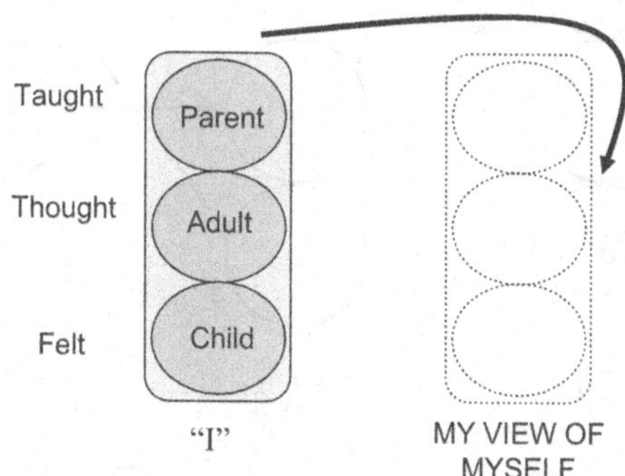

Figure 4.3 Extending the "I" in TA.

Undertaking transactions

Applying P-A-C personality framework in people management

The "I" persona engages in interactions with others, which consist of a stimulus from one person and a response from the other. These interactions are known as transactions. In Agile projects, there are numerous daily transactions, as individuals and their interactions are essential. The Parent-Adult-Child (P-A-C) grid applies to each transaction, regardless of whether it is a brief exchange of pleasantries or a more complex conversation with a superior. While some transactions may be resolved quickly, others may require a more extended discussion period and may not always be verbal. For example, a transaction between the two parties "A" and "B" such as "G'day, how is it going?" – "Fine, thanks!" completes within a few seconds. Such a transaction is a courtesy offered to each other and contains no substantial work-related information. This is a complimentary transaction with parallel lines reaching a satisfactory conclusion within seconds.

Figure 4.4 shows the rules of the transaction, which are that so long as the initiation and response lines of a transaction are running parallel to each other, a transaction is complimentary, and it can continue without friction. However, should a response be "Get out of my way!" as also shown in Figure 4.4 on the right, then the transactions are crossed, and communication

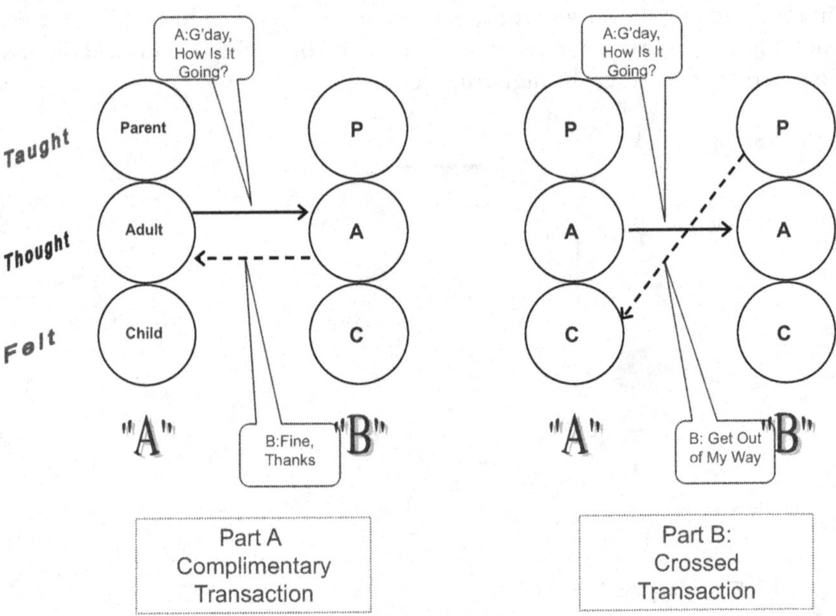

Figure 4.4 Complimentary and Crossed Transactions.

between the two parties cannot continue anymore. Figure 4.4 further shows that transactions are complimentary (P → C to C → P; or A ↔ A) when the ego states are complimenting each other. These complimentary transactions need not be always from A to A. For example, a colleague experiencing a "low" due to poor work product (Child ego state) may need a supportive leader who can explain the errors and provide positive stroking for future good work (Parent ego state). However, when transactions cross (P → C, P → C), there is no opportunity for ongoing communications in an agile team. Keeping the "Adult" in charge of stimuli and response provides maximum opportunity to avoid crossed transactions.

The rules of complementary transactions also apply to more in-depth interactions, such as one initiated with the boss: "When will I be getting my bonus? or "I found a couple of cybersecurity risks in the Python code written by Joe." This stimulus requires a long, drawn-out response by the boss over a considerable period of time. This kind of transaction can extend over days and may not always happen through words. Once again, awareness of the multiple ego states and bringing out a more experienced and mature Adult ego state into play can bring such a transaction to a satisfactory completion.

The concept of P-A-C and its application in various Agile ceremonies, including the daily stand-up meeting, can greatly enhance team performance. Given the time constraints of these meetings (15 minutes max), team members need to adopt an Adult ego state and minimize the expressions of the Child ego state, which can lead to frivolity in the meetings. Excessive use of the Parent ego state can also lead to unproductive meetings. For example, a team member with a "Parent" ego state may keep looking at their watch every minute to see if the daily stand-up actually finishes in the prescribed 15 minutes or not. Prioritizing the Adult ego state in these meetings keeps the underlying philosophy of agile in mind and, therefore, leads to higher productivity and better-quality outcomes.

The social interactions depicted in Figure 4.4 occur between two individuals and can be applied to larger groups such as teams, organizations, and nations. This is because teams and organizations, like individuals, also possess unique identities. In addition, the interplay between these entities can expand to encompass numerous individuals, teams, organizations, and nations.

LIFE POSITIONS AND AGILE TEAM COLLABORATION

Figure 4.5 highlights how these life positions can shape agile team structures – from rigid and hierarchical to synchronous teams. The life positions are not fleeting emotions but rather a central theme in a person that develops in childhood and acts as a psychological foundation for the rest of one's life. Despite the many challenges one may face including a possible miserable situation at work or home, an individual will be unconsciously guided

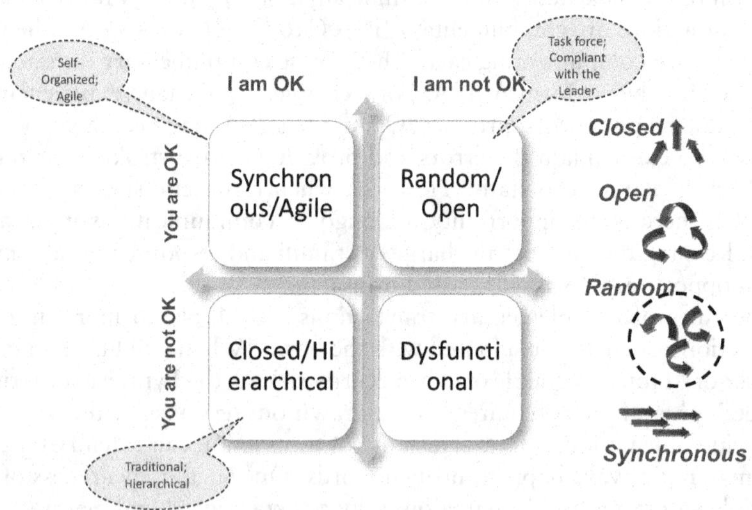

Figure 4.5 TA Life Positions and Agile Team Structures.

by his or her life position. Individuals will also defend their life position formed in early childhood irrespective of the outcomes it produces because it provides a sense of psychological security. Life positions impact the way day-to-day experiences are perceived and heavily influence transactions. Decision-making, communications, and relationships are all influenced by life positions. As an Agile leader, understanding how life positions affect interactions is crucial. This is so because an OK life position will enable the individual to bring out his Adult ego state more often. In contrast, a recording of Not-OK will inadvertently switch the individual to either Parent (to defend his or her viewpoint) or Child (to be sad or angry at their viewpoint not being recognized). Life positions are our childhood conclusions about life, which are recorded deep within the memory mechanism. These recordings are so deep and in the distant past for most working individuals that it may be practically impossible to recollect them or remember them. However, the theory of TA says that these recordings are *relived* in the present, affecting the daily transactions and working environments. Awareness of the life positions and the ego states is a constructive and positive way to identify and overcome limiting beliefs and work toward positive and productive relationships. The TA framework suggests four specific life positions that can impact Agile teams. These four life positions are as follows:

I am not OK – You are OK: the most commonly formed decision by a child that stays with him/her for the rest of life.

I am OK – You are not OK: a childhood rebellious decision that produces authoritative and autocratic leadership based on a false sense of security.

I am OK – You are OK: The winner's life decision provides immense value to everyone around such a person. Parents and teachers need to coax children into this decision in early childhood.

I am not OK – You are not OK: is a futile decision or a complete lack of decision that leads to incoherence and incoordination in life. It is an unlikely scenario in Agile projects and more of a clinical psychiatry topic.

The following discussion expands on the life positions and how they impact the Agile workplace.

I am not OK; you are OK

In the "I am not OK; You are OK" life position, a team member may feel deeply ingrained inferiority, leading to an "Adaptive Child" ego state that can result in frivolous, fearful, and uncertain behavior in daily work transactions. While the Child ego state can contribute to the fun and relaxed atmosphere of Agile teams, it should be controlled by a functioning Adult ego state. As team members work to overcome the Not-OK position, they may experience resistance and game-playing with authority figures, damaging trust and honesty within the team. Agile leaders should be aware of this universal life position, both in themselves and their team members, and seek external help to overcome the impact of negative memories.

I am OK; you are not OK

The "I am OK; you are not OK" life position is based on a feeling of superiority that hinders collaboration and communication among team members. Such superiority as a life position may not always be based on childhood recordings but, in most cases, a reaction or a rebellion against the "Not-OKness" within. Leaders who rebel against their own "Not-OK" and flip to adopt this "I am OK; but you are Not OK" life position tend to have a dictatorial approach and respond from a place of superiority. The active ego state is mostly that of the Parent. While this attitude may work in traditional task-driven project management, where each task is detailed, it is not helpful in an Agile work environment. Agile work environments require leaders who treat team members equally and respectfully, which are key criteria of the Agile Manifesto. A controlling approach is not conducive to the fuzzy softness of Agile projects where work is conducted based on trust, honesty, and collaboration within the team. By developing a careful awareness of this life position within oneself, the "Adult" ego state can be activated. This activation of the Adult is the mechanism that helps a leader or team member realize that it is not necessary to make others feel Not-OK for them to feel OK. As a result, the grip on this life position can be gently released.

I am OK; you are OK

Successful leaders and motivators possess a universal attitude of respect toward themselves and others, even in the face of challenges. Maintaining a positive outlook and recognizing the value and potential of every team member is the foundation of "I am OK; you are OK." This mindset is embodied by a winning leader who fosters a collaborative and supportive work environment, empowering each team member to contribute their unique skills and perspectives. While the Adult ego state is dominant, leaders in this position also allow the Parent and Child ego states to emerge when appropriate, encouraging rules and humor at the right time and place. For example, these leaders may organize social events and after-work drinks to allow individuals to freely express their "Child" personality.

A team with this "OK" mentality has effective leadership, collaboration, mutual respect, and a clear understanding of their abilities and limitations. The leader or coach's "I am OK; you are OK" life position is critical in creating a winning Agile team. A winning team is a relaxed place to work, with an equal emphasis on happening as doing, which effortlessly produces quality outcomes. The leader, however, needs to put in effort to direct the team toward this winning life position, as childhood influences on memory mechanisms are active in the leader as in the team members. Deep awareness of these influences and open communication with trusted colleagues is one way to create an "OK" Agile environment.

I am not OK; you are not OK

The "I am not OK; you are not OK" outlook on life is a challenging position in which a team member distances themselves from the group and, in severe cases, withdraws entirely. While this behavior is not typically seen in the workplace, it can stem from traumatic events either at home or at work. When someone is in this state, they may feel vulnerable and helpless, requiring support and guidance from others to regain a sense of control. If a team has a member or leader in this position, people can't work together effectively, rendering the team dysfunctional. It is crucial to recognize that this life position requires clinical intervention and is beyond the scope of practical Agile discussions.

GAMES IN ORGANIZATIONS

This section discusses the origins of games as described in TA, relates gamey behavior to agile work environments and discusses how to avoid games at work. A few examples games from IT projects are presented through a game pattern.

The psychological burden of not-OK

"Stop playing games!" often expresses frustration and negativity toward certain activities. However, games like cricket, rugby, baseball, soccer, and golf can be enjoyable and positive when played as team sports in a school or backyard setting. Unfortunately, when people engage in dishonest or harmful behavior during these games, they can have a negative connotation. This is especially true in the psychological realm, where a behavior tends to be gamey when it has an underlying negative motive. Games are usually "played" in a work environment by individuals to temporarily relieve the burden of the Not-OK position of inadequacy or distress. In TA, games with hidden motivations and payoffs are called "playing games" and are detrimental to personal growth in work or social relationships. The productivity and quality of work and the joy of working that emanates from an agile work environment are put at risk due to gamey behavior.

Engaging in games is a way of structuring time at work when the productive outcomes are not apparent. Games lead to negative consequences as they are unproductive ways of structuring time. A "payoff" in a game serves as a way to structure time as it leads to further transactions even though the individuals participating in the games may carry a feeling of being lost. Games are a poor way to overcome the burden of "Not-OK." A game is a series of ulterior transactions leading to a well-defined outcome,[9] usually negative. These games often have hidden motivations and can be very harmful, particularly in the context of agile teams. Since a significant portion of our working time is spent engaging in some form of game, it is crucial to understand their nature.

Time structuring and pay-offs

According to the theory of TA, "games" is derived from the fundamental human challenge of "how to pass time?" Structuring time through activities, rituals, hobbies, and withdrawal is common. These activities can be managed formally and structured to accomplish the underlying human motives. For instance, a person can withdraw from work while still in a crowded office or engage in a nine-to-five routine to cope with the need to structure

9 Berne, E., 1964, *Games People Play*, Penguin, New York, NY.

time. Meetings, training sessions, workshops, and other work activities are examples of formal time structuring techniques. Even informal activities like chatting in the hallway or taking a coffee break can be considered pastimes to help structure time. Time structuring can be a formal and rigid process, or it can be relaxed and fun, depending on the specific needs and goals of the individual.

When people engage in different relationships, such as friendships, software projects, marriages, or parliaments, they exhibit certain behavioral patterns that fit with their stimulus-response mechanisms. These patterns ensure they continue participating in the relationship, even if it is miserable. Berne suggests that in most cases, a divorce or a car crash is the ultimate "payoff" of a series of moves made by different "players" participating in a "game." This game is driven by psychological "payoffs," highlighting the poignant human tragedy of the compulsion to "play games."

Relating games to agile workplace

Games often happen when humans interact with each other. Agile work environments are characterized by rich human interactions. Agility emphasizes the importance of individuals and their interactions, the ability to create a functional solution rather than just a theoretical concept, collaboration with customers rather than just following contractual agreements, and an acceptance of change as inevitable and welcome.

Ego states and life positions provide the right context for discussing games within an Agile work environment. When a leader exhibits their Adult ego state, which comes from the winner's life position of "I am OK; You are OK," the work environment has minimal games and maximum productivity with quality. The Parent ego state suggests minimal but valuable rules and protocols, while the Child ego state permits laughter and fun. The Parent is also valuable in providing continuity of work experience (based on experiences derived from previous iterations in a typical agile environment) and balancing it with permissions for emotional expressions of the Child ego state. Thus, the personas are balanced in a productive, agile environment with the Adult in charge of the transactions. Figure 4.6 shows this balancing aspect of Parent-Adult-Child (P-A-C) succinctly. The Adult is in charge of transactions in a game-free environment but both Parent and Child contribute significantly to an agile workplace.

In contrast, when the leader or team members operate from the most common life position of "I am not OK; You are OK," it can lead to gamey behavior. Games in an Agile work environment range from developing endless requirements for a product and utilizing every available feature of technology to suffering from unproductive meetings and developing the bravery to face failures rather than avoiding them. The tools, practices, and collaborations are out of sync in a gamey work environment.

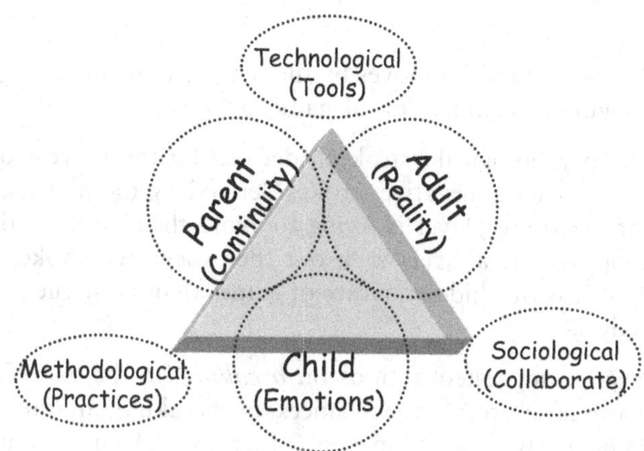

Figure 4.6 Keeping P-A-C in Balance – Antidote to Games.

A game pattern

This section further explores games frequently played out in IT projects and suggests ways to counteract them. A game pattern provides a structure to describe and understand games. This is followed by a few examples from IT games. A workplace is inundated with numerous games. Understanding each and every game at work is not possible, nor necessary. Once the theme behind games is understood through these examples, it becomes easier to spot games at work. The antidotes to the games, as suggested here, are also not prescriptive. Astute agile leaders will come up with their own variations to the suggestions here to sidestep or break gamey behaviors. Further discussions and practical applications of these concepts in varying work environments will ensure the effective handling of gamey behaviors and open up doors to authentic creativity and quality outcomes.

A GAME PATTERN

Following is a game pattern that succinctly describes a game:

Name of the Game: <Name and general description that is helpful in referring to the game at work>
Players:

<Red: A person initiating the game by starting a stimulus that eventually snowballs into a game

Green: A person responding to the stimulus by Red, and who is usually instrumental in the early moves in the game. This person is more likely to be at the receiving end of the game

Patsy: Person or persons who are simple bystanders inadvertently embroiled in the games.>

Moves: <The usual standard moves by the players that starts the game and leads to an ongoing enactment of the game. >

Payoffs: <The psychological "strokes" derived by the players due to the game. These are usually negative strokes derived by the players, although that does not mean the player is trying to avoid them. In fact, the players may unconsciously yet actively seek out these negative strokes based on their positions. It is this hidden nature of games that led Berne to call them human tragedy. >

Antidote: < Some suggested options on *breaking up* the games. If moves by players are understood, the chances of breaking up the games by not responding to the moves increase, thereby reducing game playing. Developing an active Adult ego state from which to respond is an important element in breaking up games. >

Analysis:

The analysis is a discussion of the game to better understand it. The key to comprehending games and avoiding undesirable outcomes is a curative approach that emphasizes awareness. The Adult ego state with its capability for reality-testing is most cognizant of the game's mechanics. Therefore, the Adult ego state functioning out of the "I am OK; You are OK" life position lowers the likelihood of engaging in game playing.

Use it or lose it

Name of the Game: Use it or lose it

Players:

Red: Developer – responsible for putting together a slice of the solution; over enthusiastic "techie"

Green: Team leader – assuming responsibility for the solution; Indirectly encourages while overtly discouraging

Patsy: Other team members

Moves: 1. Red incorporates all available features in a tool or technology in the solution that he is developing.

2. Green observes what Red is doing with a feeling that there is no need to use all the features available for the solution release

3. Patsys observe indirectly and makes no comments.

4. Red creates a release of the solution that is bulky, slow and likely to be difficult to maintain

5. Green goes ahead with the release

6. The release FAILS

Payoffs: Red: "I gave it a good try"; Green: "I told you so" (even though it was not told).

Antidote:

Red to use only the bare minimum tool and technology feature as needed for the solution release; Green to actually tell him that all features of a tool are not required; Patsys can intervene if their Parent allows them to

The antidote to this "Use It or Lose It" game comes from leaders who understand the importance of limiting the use of technology features that are not necessary. They prioritize quality meetings and workshops incorporating designs that undergo thorough quality checks. This ensures that every component feature or use case request aligns with a genuine need in the problem space. Justification is the key to avoiding this game. Although generalization in object designs is necessary for product reusability, it can also be complex. Those who generalize for reuse should remain objective and in an Adult ego state, thus avoiding unnecessary generalization.

Analysis

In the world of AI, developers may be tempted to use every feature available in their development environment simply because it seems impressive. However, this approach often leads to unnecessary complexity and can overwhelm users. Decades ago, Brown et al. [1998][10] discussed the software architecture antipattern of a Swiss knife, where a class or component has hundreds of interfaces to handle any possible situation. Many of these features may be included simply because the language offers and a developer wants to insert them in their solution. Awareness of this situation and focusing on the bare minimum use of available features is the antidote to this game. Prioritizing user stories and tasks based on their importance so that the most important work gets done first, even if the team faces unexpected issues also ensures that time is not wasted in using a technology feature if it does not provide value in developing a user story. Keeping the Adult ego state active in deciding on the use of features and controlling the child-like tendency of using a thing only because it is "cool" is part of the antidote.

10 Brown, W. J., Malveau, R., McCormick, S., and Mowbray, T., 1998, *AntiPatterns: Refactoring Software, Architectures, and Projects in Crisis*, John Wiley & Sons, Hoboken, NJ.

Flour mix

Name of the Game: Flour Mix

Players:

Red: Developer – a well-meaning person who wants to provide the best possible word product

Green: Product Owner or Business Analyst – who wants to have the best possible solution for the users

Patsy: Business stakeholders (others)

Moves: 1. Developer creates and demonstrates a feature that the Product Owner had asked for in a User Story

2. The Product Owner applauds the results, indicating that the feature required in the solution works.

3. The Product Owner then casually mentions another feature that would have made the current release of the product absolutely great.

4. The Patsys do not highlight any urgency even if it may be there in terms of releasing the current slice of the solution

5. Developer tries to add that additional feature even though the current release is ready to go.

6. Adding the new feature DELAYS the release

Payoffs: Release is delayed or fails.

Antidote:

As an antidote to this game, it is recommended that once a set of functionalities is laid out on a Kanban board or use case diagram, the team should aim to provide those functionalities in the first release. Modifying the use cases or class diagrams is permissible, but any resulting scope changes should be addressed in a later release. Employing a time-boxed development approach, with releases due every three months or so, can also help mitigate this game. Additionally, if a feature is required, it is accepted under the condition that it will be provided in the subsequent release. Dedicating part of the team's capacity to address unexpected events is most helpful in accepting changes without adding to planned work. Previous iteration's performance in terms of team velocity is also helpful in keeping this game in check as the data can directly indicate the need to avoid adding features in the current release. Green needs to avoid making casual aspirational comments that stem from the Child ego state, while Red should refrain from getting caught up in satisfying those comments.

Analysis

The concept of flour mix is a familiar topic in IT project management, often referred to as the "creep factor." It's a game played by developers, sometimes with the help of project managers, where they want to add one more feature with genuine intent before delivering the system. However, to meet this goal, they require more time and resources. The development process becomes akin to an inexperienced cook mixing water and flour to create bread dough. Initially, the mix may not work out, resulting in extra water. To compensate, the cook adds more flour, leading to dry dough, and the cycle continues indefinitely.

Meetingitis

Name of the Game: Meetingitis

Players:

Red: Team Leader

Green: Team Members

Patsy: Administrative support/Others

Moves:

1. Team Leader conducts a good, productive meeting.
2. Team Leader announces the meeting is over.
3. Then Red, the Team Leaders asks if "anyone has any questions?"
4. Green, one of the Team members, asks a quick, casual questions. He also mentions that this is a quick question.
5. Red, the Team Leader gets "sucked" into the question and provides a detailed answer that includes information that is far more than what was asked
6. Green, the other Team member, asks a follow up question.
7. Red answers to that specific Team member while the entire team, which has not much to do with the question, continues to listen

Payoffs: Red – feels that he did a great job of answering one last question but, in reality, wasted time of team members; Green feels it was a quick question that had to be asked. Patsys are not brave enough to jump in and end the wasteful part of the meeting and end up wasting their own time.

Antidote:

One effective antidote to unproductive meetings is establishing an agenda beforehand and re-reiterating it within the first five minutes of the meeting. Implementing a "parking lot" for off-topic issues or casual questions and comments can help keep the meeting focused. In addition to the in-person meetings, additional electronic channels of communication that opened up during the COVID-19 pandemic should be considered for topics that are specific to a person. Attendees should be encouraged to come prepared by reviewing the agenda and considering potential solutions. Highlighting that the meetings are for decision-making, not research or investigation, is also an effective antidote. Conduct regular retrospectives at the end of each iteration to review what went well and what didn't improves the accuracy of future iteration planning. The iteration planning process also provides all team members a comprehensive perspective on the work and reduces wasteful meetings during the iteration. Awareness of the unproductive meeting "game" is the first step in addressing it.

Analysis

A well-known problem in projects is that the development team spends hours in meetings without deciding on anything or resolving any issues. Agile projects are no exception. This game is a wasteful tool for structuring time for team members who don't know what to do with their time or are restless. Once they are in a meeting, even though the main goal of the meeting has been accomplished, these team members are wondering what they will do next with their time. The situation is unproductive and self-defeating and has been dubbed as a project disease of "Meetingitis" by Myer.[11] Scott Adams' cartoon character Dilbert[12] is popular because the joke comes from our personal experiences of knowing "what a waste that meeting was," and in that same breath, we are setting up another meeting for next week.

Clear blind spot

Name of the Game: Clear Blind Spot

Players:

Red: Project Leader

Green: User

Patsy: Team members

11 For more discussion, see Meyer, B. (1995), *Object Success: A Manager's Guide to Object-Oriented Technology and Its Impact on the Corporation.* Prentice Hall, Englewood Cliffs, NJ.

12 Adams, S. (1996), *The Dilbert Principle: A Cubicle's-Eye View of Bosses, Meetings, Management Fads & Other Workplace Afflictions*, HarperBusiness, New York, NY.

Moves:

1. Red, the Project Leader states that he can clearly see the problem
2. Green, the User sees that it is actually a blind spot
3. For some reason that Green cannot explain (Child ego state), she does not point out the blind spot
4. Red assumes that because no one has a contrary opinion what he sees is exactly what it is
5. Patsys see no reason to highlight the problem in a different, more correct light
6. The problem or the Blind spot in the project remains

Payoffs: Failure of a project initiative. Red feels surprised at the apparent fact that he could see the problem clearly and still he could not handle it; Green feels she should have pointed out the reality of the problem but feels it was not worth the trouble; the Patsys bear the fallout from the failure.

Antidote: Visibility of blind spots within any initiative is the antidote of handling this game. Each player in the game needs to be aware of the potential influence of their Parent-ego state, which insists that it knows the best despite the contrary facts; and the influence of the Child-ego state which prevents highlighting the errors out of fear or respect towards the Parent.

Analysis

There's a subtle difference between how clear something seems and how clear it actually is. It takes an Adult ego state to navigate and distinguish the two, otherwise the work environment can become fraught with tension and unproductive efforts. Leaders who are driven by their Parent ego may also experience insecurity stemming from their inner Child. To overcome these obstacles, it's crucial to be aware of how different ego states can influence our decisions and to cultivate a sense of inner confidence that allows us to seek honest feedback on project challenges.

MYERS–BRIGGS AND TA

The previous chapter covered the Myers–Briggs personality Test Indicator (MBTI), which provide insights into an individual's persona. This chapter outlined the P-A-C ego states, which define an individual's psychological makeup. The psychology of agile emphasizes using such tools to enhance the effectiveness of Agile teams. However, it's important to note that a single framework may not be sufficient to change one's mindset. This is because the personalities of the team members and leaders responsible for driving change differ and may require different frameworks to be effective. Therefore, it is recommended to apply multiple personality frameworks when individuals, teams, and organizations transition to an Agile work style.

Figure 4.7 depicts how the P-A-C and MBTI frameworks align and shows that the strategic-tactical and planned-agile pairs are on a continuum influenced by the individual and team's transition. For example, Thinking and Judging are almost exclusively Parent ego state characteristics. Feeling and Perceiving, on the other hand, are Child ego state characteristics. As individuals attempt to understand the reality, their personality type and ego state influence their attempts. Table 4.1 briefly maps each MBTI indicator

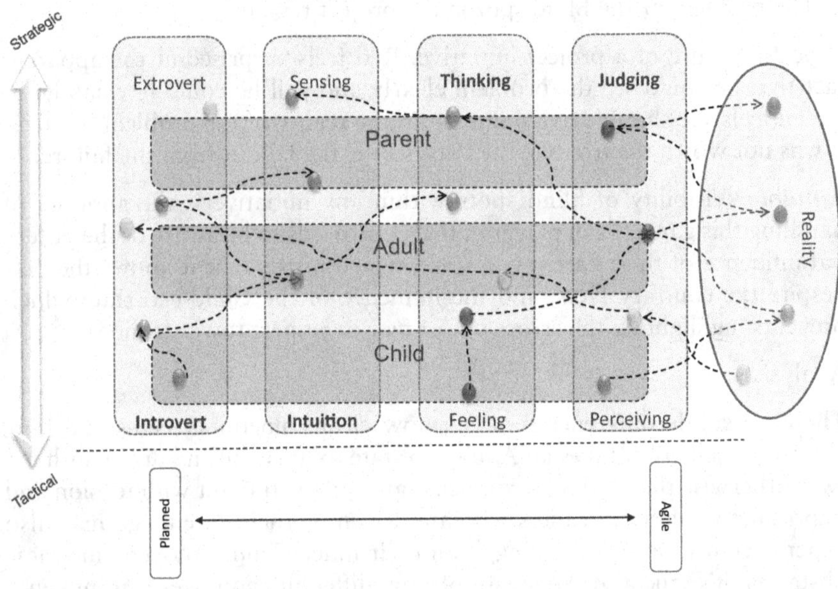

Figure 4.7 Myers–Briggs and TA Mapping.

Table 4.1 Mapping MBTI Elements with P-A-C

MBTI	*Dominant Ego State*		
	Parent	*Adult*	*Child*
Extrovert			X
Introvert	X		
Sensing		X	
Intuition			X
Thinking		X	
Feeling			X
Judging	X		
Perceiving		X	

and the corresponding dominant ego state. Increasing awareness of the ego states leads to an improved understanding of one's personality type and vice versa. The key to successful intra- and inter-team interactions is to keep the Adult ego state in charge of whatever is happening.

CONSOLIDATION WORKSHOP

1. Can you explain how you understand the TA framework and its significance in an agile work environment? Include your brief understanding of ego states, life positions, and games as key elements of TA.
2. How would you define the term persona? Please discuss the relationship between memory mechanisms and persona. Could you elaborate on how a persona comprises three "I" or egos at a fundamental level?
3. Could you briefly outline the key characteristics of the three ego states of TA and provide examples of how an individual may act in each of these ego states?
4. What is a social transaction in the context of TA? Could you act out a response to the same stimulus, such as "Do you need assistance with that user story you're working on?" from each of the three ego states and compare the responses?
5. Can you explain what the life position in TA is? How is it different from a sense or a feeling?
6. Discuss why the "I am OK; You are OK" is the universal life position of a good leader. Your answer can include examples of comparison with the other two life positions of relevance discussed in this chapter.
7. How did the life positions of TA apply to individuals, agile teams, and agile organizations? Can a team or an organization also exhibit a life position? Include the concept of "Gestalt" in your answer.
8. What is a game? How can a game help structure time? Please include an example using the game pattern in your discussion.
9. Why are games not regarded positively in the TA community? Include the burden of "not OK" in your discussion.
10. What is a payoff in a game? Why is the payoff negative?
11. What actions can a competent leader take to break or sidestep games?
12. What is the mapping between MBTI and the TA ego states? Discuss with examples.

Chapter 5

Maslow's hierarchy and "right-brained," "slow-thinking" agile

CHAPTER SUMMARY

This chapter explores how Maslow's hierarchy of needs can be applied to an Agile workplace. The needs of human beings, including physiological, safety, love/belonging, esteem, and self-actualization, provide an excellent basis to guide the transition to an Agile approach. This chapter also explores the Composite Agile Method and Strategy (CAMS), which strikes a balance between planned processes and the flexible nature of Agile. The chapter discusses how CAMS can address different needs: planned processes aligning with physiological and safety needs, while Agile approaches align with esteem and self-actualization. The chapter also draws on the theories of Nobel laureates Roger W. Sperry ("Left-Right brains") and Daniel Kahneman (Fast and Slow thinking) to derive insights for balance. The chapter will be of immense interest and relevance for Agile leaders and team members looking to understand how to create an Agile workplace while maintaining a balance between planned processes and a flexible, fuzzy approach.

INTRODUCTION

Understanding and positively influencing work culture is a crucial responsibility of the psychology of Agile. Work culture encompasses team members' personalities, behavior, work style, communication, productivity, and exit patterns. Traditional project management approaches relied on the iron triangle of measures: time, budget, and scope, which worked well when most work was carried out in a linear, planned manner. However, in the digital age, most work carried out in organizations like banks, airlines, insurance companies, hospitals, and farms is iterative and incremental. The digital solutions that enable and support decision-making in organizations are also developed and deployed iteratively and incrementally. In such a scenario, the intangible aspects of a workplace, like morale, motivation, and

DOI: 10.1201/9781003201540-5

creativity, assume greater importance than the tangible measures of costs, time, and benefits.

Based on the Agile Manifesto, the Agile philosophy emphasizes delivering value to the customer or end user. This value is subjective and varies depending on the user's needs, which can change depending on the context. Therefore, factors that impact workplace morale, motivation, and creativity, such as flattened, collaborative, and cross-functional team structures, social events at the workplace, an unhurried workplace, and the role of authentic humor at work, become prominent. However, measuring these factors is difficult as they don't fit into known work metrics.

The discussions in this chapter start with Maslow's hierarchy of needs at work, which provides five levels of human evolution. The chapter also highlights the theories of Roger W. Sperry ("Left-Right brains") and Daniel Kahneman (Fast and Slow thinking) and maps them to Maslow's needs hierarchy. This chapter further provides the basis for understanding and applying the CAMS as a balancing act in practice.

MASLOW'S NEEDS HIERARCHY AND AGILE

Abraham Maslow's hierarchy of needs[1] provides a useful framework to understand evolution of human needs. Basic needs like food and security must be met before higher-level needs such as belongingness and self-esteem can be fulfilled. These needs change as individuals mature and gain more experience at work. For instance, while a secure and comfortable workplace is important for a young team member, someone with decades of experience values more self-esteem. The psychology of Agile involves integrating human needs and values with corresponding workplace needs. As a leader, it is critical to consider how team members' needs might impact their work. For example, team members who are worried about safety may be less productive or engaged. On the other hand, team members who have a sense of belonging and connection with their colleagues will likely be more motivated and invested in their work. Addressing these concerns and providing reassurance and encouragement is essential for agile leadership.

Agile leaders foster a sense of belonging for their team members through various techniques that create trust based on open communication and collaboration and a demonstrated "I am OK; You are OK" life position. Agile leaders use Maslow's needs hierarchy to prioritize what is important to team members. The hierarchy of needs recognizes the different levels of human needs and how they impact team members' behavior. In doing so, leaders can prioritize and customize team members' needs to create a work environment that fosters trust, communication, and collaboration, resulting in

1 **Maslow's hierarchy of needs** is a theory in psychology proposed by Abraham Maslow in his 1943 paper "A Theory of Human Motivation."

improved team performance. This needs pyramid evolves from basic human needs of survival to self-actualization. Individuals progress and grow on these needs to eventually reach their full potential.

The theory suggests that individuals strive to fulfill their basic physiological and safety needs before advancing to more complex needs such as esteem and self-actualization. This hierarchy is a reference point for leaders to comprehend the evolving human motivation and behavior. Once the work environment transcends the basic human needs and moves into the realms of belonging and esteem, the fundamentals of Agile, its manifesto, and agile values take extraordinary precedence. Each of the five levels in the needs hierarchy is discussed next in the context of an Agile work environment.

Physiology needs and agile

In modern work environments, it's generally assumed that team members' basic physiological needs are met. These needs are crucial for maintaining productivity and engagement, so leaders ensure they're easily satisfied. Necessities like drinking water, coffee, and restroom facilities, along with comfortable workspaces and ergonomic equipment prevent discomfort and injury. When teams work intensely, these needs become more critical, as some team members may ignore them in the heat of their work. In an agile work environment, teams work extremely collaboratively. Meeting these basic needs ensures the agile team can work without disruptions. Despite their significance, these basic needs are often overlooked and taken for granted, as most of them are usually satisfied. Keeping an eye on these needs is a good starting point for evolving the team along the Maslow's needs hierarchy.

Safety needs and agile

The second layer of Maslow's hierarchy of needs focuses on team members' safety and security needs. This means that individuals should feel physically safe in their work environment and be protected from harassment, discrimination, and other similar workplace issues. While employees' perceptions of safety and security may differ, these needs are generally well defined in modern-day workplaces. While it is not solely the agile leader's responsibility to fulfill these needs, they can ensure fairness and equality through training and leveraging additional resources to identify potential safety hazards and prevent accidents. Regular safety drills, updated first-aid kits, and emergency response plans are activities that HR can undertake to prioritize safety in the workplace. Agile teams are diverse and have a mix of cultures, especially when work is outsourced or off-shored. An Agile work environment can be supportive, productive, and sustainable by prioritizing safety and creating a distraction-free environment. Satisfying this second layer of Maslow's hierarchy of needs opens doors for moving to the next layer.

Belonging needs and agile

A sense of belonging is crucial in any human endeavor, especially in an agile team environment. This is mainly because Agile is a collaborative team effort that comes into play after the physiological and safety needs are satisfied. Belonging is thus the important third layer in Maslow's needs hierarchy. While "belonging" is the key to forming social structures, this need assumes further importance in an Agile environment. The relative absence of a "carrot and stick" approach in an Agile environment means that the leader in such an environment must create situations that foster the feeling of belongingness. This third layer of needs becomes more difficult to measure than the previous two because belongingness is subjective. When the leader handles this need for belongingness, the team members are encouraged to be self-organized and self-managed. Individuals feel enthused enough to start taking more responsibility for their work, share the tasks that support each other, and work synchronously toward a common goal. Leaders of cross-functional teams, typically all Agile teams, need "belonging" more as they collaborate with team members from various professional backgrounds and differing value systems. For example, a developer, a tester, a product owner, and an accounting advisor may be on the same Agile team, demanding a greater need for belonging than a mono-functional or traditional project team. A good Agile leader will continuously appreciate and value individual team members' contributions and encourage individuals to appreciate each other's contributions. Team-building activities, regular and specifically targeted communication, and visibility of work engender a sense of belonging. Assuming joint responsibility by the team invariably leads to an increased sense of belongingness.

Esteem needs and agile

Healthy self-esteem is crucial for one's psychological well-being. It also plays a critical role in personal success and the success of an agile team environment. According to Maslow's hierarchy of needs, self-esteem is at the fourth level, emphasizing individuals' over processes. This importance aligns closely with the very first statement of the Agile Manifesto: "Individuals and interactions over processes and tools." For Agile leaders, recognizing the role of self-esteem in the workplace is vital in creating a supportive and productive environment. Agile practices promote belongingness among team members through collaboration but also encourage self-mastery of the skills necessary at the project and organizational levels. Team members with healthy self-esteem feel appreciated and respected, leading to greater ownership and self-mastery, which produces a sense of pride in contributing to the team's success. This positive attitude reduces competition and fosters a relaxed and enjoyable work environment, resulting in collaboration and teamwork, essential for agile projects to succeed. Team members with healthy self-esteem understand the importance of avoiding harmful behaviors. At the "belonging" level of Maslow's hierarchy, Agile is free of "gamey" behaviors, and the leader and team members primarily transact through their Agile ego state.[2]

Self-actualization needs and agile

Self-actualization, the fifth layer of Maslow's hierarchy of needs, is the most rewarding and yet the most complex. The reason for the complexity of this final layer of the needs hierarchy is multifaceted, encompassing both physical and spiritual elements. Self-actualization involves a deep understanding of one's unique talents, abilities, and potential and a gentle wish to let it flourish without competition and undue effort. Self-actualization results from a deep inner balance and a relaxed, unhurried approach to work and life. Awareness of oneself, mindfulness of one's actions, and universality of respect are the key components of reaching this highest potential of self-actualization in the workplace and in life. Spiritual Intelligence (SI) may be the term that describes these aforementioned characteristics. However, going into the formal definition of SI is out of the scope of this discussion. Attempts to define SI would also fall short primarily because SI is the inner core of human experience that is a felt rather than a thought capability. Individuals with strong SI often see beyond the surface level of things and can arrange and rearrange themselves at a deeper, more meaningful level, especially in team environments.

In an agile work environment, a leader who is also agile can dynamically rearrange their team with minimum friction and promote enjoyable collaborative work. As individuals develop strong SI, they approach tasks in a non-competitive and unhurried manner while supporting, inspiring, and motivating their fellow team members. With each iteration or sprint, team members feel an ever-increasing sense of satisfaction as they progress toward their objectives. The ultimate layer of self-actualization, which emphasizes "being" rather than "becoming," enables the "Be-Happen" described in Chapter 1 (Figure 1.2). Therefore, level 5 represents the highest possibility of evolution at work, resulting in the highest quality of outcomes that remain beyond measurement.

2 Unhelkar, B., 1998, "Transactional Analysis (TA) as Applied to the Human Factor in Object-Oriented Projects," *The Handbook of Object Technology* (Ed. Saba Zamir), CRC Press, Boca Raton, USA (Chapter 42).

MAPPING MASLOW'S NEEDS HIERARCHY AND LEFT- AND RIGHT-BRAINED BEHAVIORS IN AGILE

This section presents an additional perspective on Maslow's needs hierarchy by exploring the potential benefits an agile leader can derive from considering it in light of the theory of left and right brains. As a staged evolution of an individual's needs, the hierarchy provides a useful framework for understanding a person's motivations and drives. At the same time, the theory of left and right brains offers insights into how cognitive processes affect our behavior and decision-making. By combining these two approaches, agile leaders can further understand their team members' needs and perspectives to build effective, adaptive work environments.

The theory of right brain-left brain dominance was introduced by Nobel laureate Roger W. Sperry.[3] This theory suggests that people dominated by the left brain are analytical, logical, and comfortable with numbers. They tend to work from detailed parts to the whole and excel in tasks that involve planning and organizing metrics and measures. Their primary ego state is the Parent, superimposed by Adult. Compared to this, those with dominant right brains tend to be holistic, using their visual, imaginative, and spatial abilities effectively. Right brain dominant personalities excel in tasks requiring creativity and intuition such as brainstorming and envisioning. Right-brained behaviors are characterized by a focus on the whole rather than the parts and their primary ego state is Child, superimposed by Adult. Physiologically, the left brain controls the right part of the body, and vice versa.[4]

As individuals move up Maslow's hierarchy of needs, their work shifts from concrete, measurable parameters to more abstract and difficult-to-measure concepts. This shift is similar to moving from left-brained, analytical tasks to right-brained, creative pursuits. Figure 5.1 shows this evolution of an individual from the base layers of Maslow's needs hierarchy, dominated by the left, analytical brain, to the effable layer of self-actualization dominated by the right, creative brain. Professions like engineering and accounting tend to be left brained, while teaching and counseling are more right brained. Programming tasks in software projects are left brained because they are based on the given syntax, whereas capturing requirements on a user story and discussing them with the product owner are right-brained tasks. Awareness of the characteristics of the two halves of the brain helps in using both sides of the brain effectively, as needed. Effective agile leaders exercise their brain halves as needed and also carefully relate to their team members'

3 Sperry, R. W., "The Future of Psychology," *The American Psychologist*, 1995, 50(7), pp. 505–506.

4 For further discussions on lateralization of brain functions see: Gazzaniga, M. S., Ivry, R. B., & Mangun, G. R. *Cognitive Neuroscience: The Biology of the Mind*. 4th ed., W.W. Norton & Company, 2013, New York, NY.

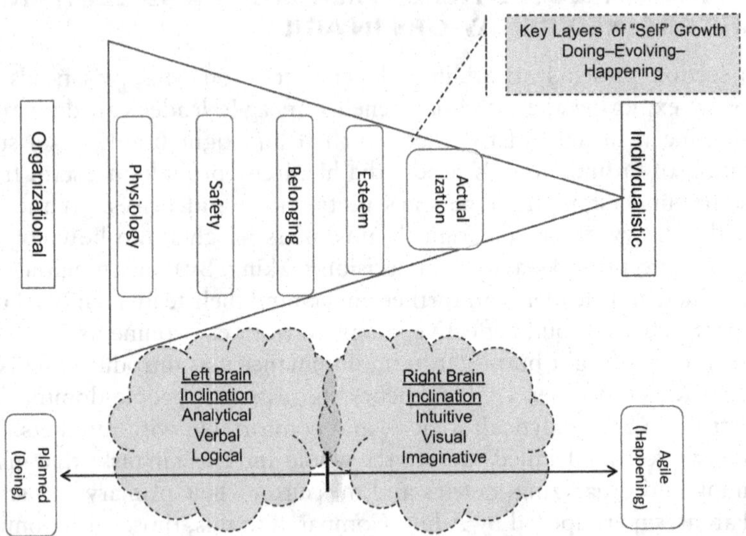

Figure 5.1 Maslow's Need Hierarchy, the Left and Right Brain, and the Place of Agile.

dominating brains. Table 5.1 provides an overview of the mapping of Maslow's hierarchy to software project lifecycles and corresponding impacts teams and organizations.

Figure 5.1 further shows that an Agile work environment shifts significantly toward utilizing the right brain. To elaborate on this point, Figure 5.1 superimposes the "left-right brain" characteristics onto Maslow's hierarchy, drawn horizontally to illustrate the progression from left-brained to right-brained characteristics.[5]

A common joke that accountants prioritize cost over value holds some truth. Accounting and finance professionals often aim to trim what appears to be unnecessary expenses, such as team-building exercises, educational seminars, and celebratory gatherings. Although these are expenses for an accounting, analytical discipline, cutting them can negatively affect team spirit and creativity, corresponding with intuitive and imaginative thinking.

The right-brain emphasis comes with its own set of challenges. As we move toward the right side of Figure 5.1, the circumstances become more adaptable but less precise. The fuzziness of the right brain increases the level of risk involved. While flexibility allows for greater potential to adjust and evolve, change is often met with resistance as it inevitably brings about risks

5 Unhelkar, B., *The Psychology of Agile: Fundamentals beyond the Manifesto,* Cutter Executive Report, Dec 2013, Vol. 14, No. 5, Agile Product & Project Management Practice, Cutter, Boston, USA; Unhelkar, B., *The Psychology of Agile-II: Group Dynamics and Organizational Adoption,* Cutter Executive Report, Oct 2015, Vol. 16, No. 4, Boston, USA.

Table 5.1 Mapping Maslow's Human Needs Hierarchy, Left-Right Brains, Project Lifecycles, Teams and Organizational Structures

Maslow's Needs	*Left/Right Brain (Primarily)*	*Impact on Project Lifecycles*	*Impact on Project Work Environments (Teams)*	*Impact on Organizational Structures and Leadership*
Physiology	Extreme left brain	Waterfall	Extreme planned (CMM Level 5)	Hierarchical – leadership is rigid, directive, and controlling; pyramid team structure
Safety	Left brain	Spiral	Planned (CMM Level 3–4)	Hierarchical – leadership is rigid, but considers factors beyond only the physical ones; initiates some discussions with team members., directed structure
Belonging	Left-right combination	Iterative-incremental	Planned – but starts to accept changes (CMM Level 1–2)	Matrix leadership structure with some activities owned by the team members and others directed
Esteem	Right brain	Agile-composite	Anticipates and plans for changes	Flattened team structure with greater facilitation than direction by leadership; collaboration is encouraged. Loosening of control from the leader.
Actualization	Extreme right brain	Agile-composite	Welcomes and even initiates changes in all areas of work	Self-organized – self-managed, collaborative team structure. Servant-leadership in action. Leaders are pure facilitators and they protect the team/organization from external influences.

that organizations may need to prepare to handle. Agile leaders continuously need to recognize balance as integral to success in agile work environments. This balance at work is also the cornerstone of CAMS.

RIGHT-BRAINED AGILE TEAM CULTURES

In the past, project management primarily relied on a left-brained approach, emphasizing the importance of cost, time, and scope. The reason for reliance on numbers was that early software project management methods were derived from construction and manufacturing projects with rigid lifecycles. However, as the world increasingly focuses on software-intensive Machine Learning and Big Data development projects, there is a growing need for greater fluidity and less rigidity. The right-brained characteristics have become crucial in meeting this demand.

Agility at work can, therefore, be considered right brained, with a greater emphasis on facilitation and leadership rather than traditional task management. This right-brained culture is evident in Agile work, using visual charts for all to see, user stories to be discussed and developed, daily stand-ups without playing games, self-managed teams with a coach instead of a manager, and honesty and visibility throughout the project. Team members who are right brained are well synced with each other and self-organized. In Agile teams, individual contributions are emphasized over positional hierarchy. Table 5.2 summarizes these primarily right-brained Agile values in the context of their psychosociological relevance to Agile teams and organizations.

Slow and fast thinking, and CAMS

Effective agile leaders understand the value of utilizing various psychological approaches to provide diverse options and opportunities for practical application. After exploring the connection between left-right brain theory and agile leadership, this section delves into another insightful work of Nobel laureate Daniel Kahneman[6] and its relevance to agile leadership. Kahneman's theory proposes the existence of two types of thinking: fast and slow. Grasping the nuances of these two types of thinking effectively facilitates an agile work environment.

In Figure 5.2, we can see a summary of the two types of thinking systems. Fast thinking, or System 1, refers to our automatic, intuitive, and unconscious thought processes that allow for quick decision-making. This type of thinking doesn't require much cognitive effort and often involves the Child ego state superimposing on the Adult ego state during decision-making. On the other hand, slow thinking, or System 2, involves a more deliberate, fully aware, and unhurried thought process that is used for high-quality strategic

6 Kahneman, D., 2012, *Thinking, Fast and Slow*, Penguin Books, New York, NY.

Table 5.2 Right-Brained Agile Values, Their Impacts on Teams/Organizations, and Caveats for the Agile Leaders

Values (Primarily Right Brained)	*Description*	*Impact on Teams and Organizations*	*Key Considerations for Agile Leaders*
Trustworthiness	Trust among team members and between them and the leader is paramount. Consistency in responses, reliability, and a qualitative rather than quantitative approach to work engender trust. Trust also results from genuine respect for each team member and due consideration of each viewpoint.	Trust-based interactions between team members eliminates many formalities within teams. Such trust-based collaboration enables creativity and efficient problem-solving without the pressure of numbers or formal role descriptions. The intra-person friction within trust-based teams is minimum as a word is a promise and is deeply respected.	Trust is a team-based value. Therefore, the entire teams needs to move simultaneously into trust. Should only some team members demonstrate trustworthiness and others not, then the entire team fails spectacularly. The leader starts by demonstrating trustworthiness and then, gently, encourages the entire team to do so.
Simplicity	Simplicity is the ability and the desire to see artifacts without their associated paraphernalia. While most business systems today are complex, they can start as simple block diagrams and they can also be understood at various levels – the top one being simple and easy to understand.	Business systems, business strategies, data-driven decisions and human issues are all intricate and complex. Yet, by keeping the value of simplicity in mind, teams can aim to understand them at their very basic level. Once understood from a simplicity angle, they can evolve into more complex issues and yet may be easier to handle. Placing emphasis on simplicity results in improved understandability.	Simplicity does not mean the leader has to give less importance to the problems. Simplicity means the approach to handling the problems should start with simple, basic building blocks.

(continued)

Table 5.2 (Cont.)

Values (Primarily Right Brained)	*Description*	*Impact on Teams and Organizations*	*Key Considerations for Agile Leaders*
Value-focus	Value-focus is the effort made by an agile team to deliver a concrete piece of work that directly helps the user. Value-focus ensures that the work performed by the team is directed at producing results for the stakeholders. Value-focus also implies reduced focus on metrics and measurements.	A team with value-focus continuously interacts with its stakeholders in order to prioritize their values in the work being conducted. The team asks how its work will add value to the users. This value-focus engages Agile team members in productive work that benefits the end user or customer.	Values are highly subjective and they change depending on individuals, project priorities and customer needs. Leaders keep this changing value-focus in mind.
Collaboration	Collaboration is the very essence of agile teams in which team members are continuously communicating with each other, sharing responsibilities and providing support.	Collaborative teams assuming joint responsibilities for work, are based on trust for each other and make it easier for team members to work to their abilities. Team members also work collaboratively with individuals in various external roles and at different levels within the organization to achieve the common goals of a project. This collaborative approach is not limited to projects alone but extends throughout the organization, fostering collaboration between different departments and eventually leading to collaboration between organizations.	Collaboration depends on multiple factors that the agile leaders need to be aware of. Trustworthiness, simplicity and support for individual's needs by the leader help with collaboration.

Facilitation	Facilitation is a leadership characteristic that is based on providing guidance and support to the team members. Facilitation is philosophically opposite to task management.	Facilitation encourages team members to be considered as part of a flattened hierarchy and, therefore, voice their opinions, provide their inputs and work collaboratively. For agile project team members, sensitivity to project dynamics and the ability to overcome challenges through conversations, explanations, clarifications, and astute questioning are hallmarks of this value. Facilitation also includes respectful negotiation among team members for improved output.	Agile leader knows that she is a facilitator and not a manager. Therefore, there is minimal task management by a good, agile leader. Creating an environment where team members are able to produce without friction is the goal of facilitation by a leader.
Transparency	Transparency places the work of all team members up on a visual board. Team members are able to see what the entire team is doing, rather only their own work. Transparency and visibility of work goes hand in hand.	Transparency impacts teams in a positive way provided there is trust and collaboration. Transparency encourages team members to articulate their thoughts, ideas, and values clearly, unambiguously, and directly to the entire team. Transparency encourages sharing of information and skills, and also limitations that individuals might have. Transparency is the antithesis to hidden agendas. And transparency compliments trust.	Leaders need to bring a fine, balancing act in encouraging transparency in work place. Team members need to trust their leader and each other in order to be transparent. Situations where a team member is not performing well or is not being collaborative, require special leadership attention as transparency will reveal any harmful games.

(continued)

Table 5.2 (Cont.)

Values (Primarily Right Brained)	*Description*	*Impact on Teams and Organizations*	*Key Considerations for Agile Leaders*
Courage	Capability to challenge accepted norms. Also having the courage to throw away a half-baked piece of work (design) and be ready to start anew.	Courage within teams implies the ability of each team member to question the status quo and challenge the "accepted norms" within projects and organizations. Courage can play a crucial role when situations are in a "business as usual" state. Courage is invaluable in empowering individuals and teams to embrace mistakes, venture out of their comfort zones, and, ultimately, be prepared to start anew.	Leaders need to be very careful in delineating between courage and foolhardiness. There is also a thin line between the expression of courage with respect and using it to simply vent anger or dissatisfaction. Leaders themselves need to have the courage to take failures in their stride, handle challenging human-relations situation and bear the consequences of throwing away unreliable designs and product releases.
Self-Organization	Managing one's tasks with minimal or no supervision. This value enables facilitation to emerge, as opposed to the mundane task management typically undertaken in formal projects. Self-organization implies a well-synchronized team directed to project and organizational goals.	Teams with ability to self-manage without constant need for supervision are more open to sharing information, knowledge, and skills with relaxed communication mechanisms.	Leaders need to keep the complimentary values in mind in promoting and facilitating self-organization. For example, honesty and trust are most helpful in self-organizing teams, whereas lack of self-esteem in team members can degenerate the teams into a farce.
Learnability	Team members need to be able to invest time and energy into learning from each iteration and every piece of work that is created. Learnability also implies learning to improve both product and process.	Teams with learnability are continually curious, inquisitive, and in an open frame of mind. Learnability is an essential Agile value that enables team members to grow through personal	Leaders capitalize on every situation to encourage and facilitate learning for the team.

		involvement and commitment to the project. This value enables not only individual members to learn the techniques and technologies but also for the Agile coaches (and facilitators) to develop improved estimations and balanced judgments in terms of the project parameters.	
Unhurriedness	Ability to work without the time pressure while keeping the goal in the back of the mind. Developing newer capabilities and finessing existing ones as the project progresses.	Prioritizing outcomes over tasks creates the opportunity to work without time pressure. Such work environment has a different, positive gestalt that changes the quality of work. An unhurried work environment is akin to slowly and attentively cooked food as against fast food that can result in frustrations. "Go slow in order to go fast" summarizes this value.	Leaders need to astute in applying and promoting this important value. All other values discussed in this table are important for unhurriedness to work. Otherwise, this value can easily degenerate into laziness. Self-esteem and self-actualization layers in a team develops unhurriedness which supports creativity and productivity.

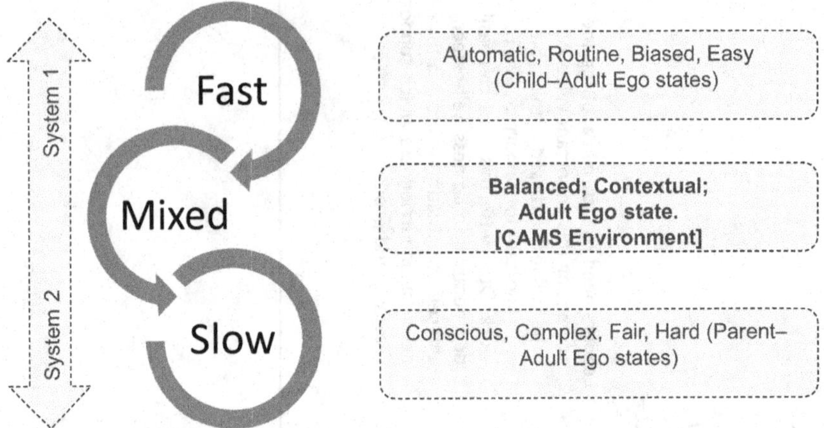

Figure 5.2 Fast and Slow Thinking in Decision-Making and CAMS.

decision-making. Understanding the differences between these two types of thinking is crucial for Agile leaders to recognize the cognitive processes that drive team dynamics. Acknowledging that both types of thinking may be necessary to support individual decision-making processes and providing the necessary support to team members forms the basis for CAMS.

Fast thinking and biases

Fast thinking, as mentioned above, is the intuitive and automatic thought process. Such a thinking process has its own place in a team and also in life. For example, in driving a car or kicking a goal, everything that is immediate and available in that instance becomes significant. There is no opportunity in such situations to go through a detailed process of considering and eliminating numerous options. The decision is rehearsed in the past, practiced to perfection, and executed instantly. The role of mental shortcuts and heuristics is crucial in such situations, even in an agile work environment. Numerous routine decisions and ensuing actions are almost automatic – starting with the quick greeting to a colleague in the morning and the walk to a daily stand-up wall. The Child ego state may superimpose over the Adult ego state in these situations.

This rapidity of thinking, however, also presents a major challenge in work environments. For example, the mental shortcuts in greeting someone take extraordinary precedence if that colleague has had a sad event in the family a few days ago. If awareness of the impact of quick decisions is low, then fast thinking can lead to biases. Race, gender, and age biases are commonplace at work, and they are a direct result of fast thinking. Fast thinking can lead to errors in judgment despite the leader believing that he or she is being rational. Fast thinking has a role to play in agile workplaces. Still, only when it is accompanied by awareness of the decisions by the leader – otherwise, fast thinking can result in irrational choices with huge negative consequences. Awareness of the biases and taking the time to reflect on the impact of decisions is most helpful in an agile workplace where so much of the work is based on communication and collaboration.

Consider, for example, a colleague suddenly asking for leave during a daily stand-up meeting. The leader has to be aware that this is a fast-thinking situation. However, a quick response based on the leader's preconceived notions can worsen the situation. Awareness of the fast-thinking part of the personality is helpful in slowing it down in terms of responding.

Consider another example where fast thinking is handy. During a work meeting, a team member was caught off guard by a question from the coach (Scrum Master). "Your user story is still in the 'doing' phase! Any problems?" The team member is aware of the delay and is also aware of the personality of the leader. So, she provides a quick response "There are couple of dependencies for this user story, I am waiting for them" – and then she has a smile on her face. This response incorporates the immediate situation and experiences of the person responding. The accompanying smile changes the gestalt of the meeting to a positive one.

Slow thinking and mindfulness

Slow thinking is a deliberate analysis of the situation that considers multiple perspectives and weighs the available options before deciding. Slow thinking further creates options that may not be apparent to the fast-thinking brain. The slow thinking process is dimensionally different from fast thinking because slow thinking is not an automatic or unconscious response to a situation. Slow thinking is generally more reliable and accurate when important decisions are made. As its name suggests, slow thinking requires significant time and effort that may not be available to everyone. In slow thinking, the Parent ego state may superimpose on the Adult ego state and, therefore, the resultant decisions would carry an aura of past decisions and value judgments.

In an agile work environment, the coach and team members benefit greatly from thinking through various factors, from technology, business, security, and performance, when developing user stories or creating iteration plans. The skill of slow thinking is essential for any activity related to iteration, sprint, or release planning. The "Retrospective" ceremony at the end of each iteration is a prime example of slow thinking, where team members reflect on the process and collaborate to refine the team's overall approach. To ensure the most effective retrospective, it's important to consider all available information carefully, conduct an unbiased evaluation, avoid cognitive biases, and create a deliberate plan for ongoing improvement.

Consider, for example, the decision on scoping an iteration in an Agile project. While an iteration is time-bound, it can take more time, effort, experience, and awareness to accurately scope it. Slow thinking process enables the team to weigh its options in close collaboration with the business and decide which features are within the scope of this particular iteration.

Another example of slow thinking is when a team member is not being productive. Consciously avoiding biases, developing an understanding of the ego states of the team member, and working through the personal challenges the team member is facing can help alleviate this situation. Slow thinking is imperative here.

Agile leaders understand the significance of both fast and slow thinking (Systems 1 and 2) in decision-making and acknowledge the importance of balancing both systems. The balance between these two systems comes with the awareness of the situation and the practice of mindfulness. Although mindfulness is typically associated with slow thinking, it can also facilitate fast decisions when the solutions are simple, and it can also help remove any biases in the decision-making process. With this deliberate approach, leaders can practice the value of unhurriedness in CAMS and make well-informed decisions.

CONSOLIDATION WORKSHOP

1. What are the five layers of Maslow's needs hierarchy, and can you provide a couple of examples from your experience for each layer?
2. Is there a role for Spiritual Intelligence in a work place? Discuss in the context of self-actualization layer of Maslow's hierarchy of needs.
3. Who developed the theory of left and right brains, and how can you interpret this theory in terms of your own experiences at work and in life? Which ego states are primarily active in each of the two halves of the brain?
4. Why are the two base layers of Maslow's needs hierarchy considered more left brained, whereas the top two are right brained? Which strategies you will develop, as a leader, to move your team from the left-brain dominance to the right-brained one?
5. Would you classify the values and fundamentals of Agile as left brained or right brained, and can you provide examples as part of your answer?
6. How can self-esteem help generate ownership, which is so crucial in an Agile project, and will it also relieve the leader from any routine or mundane tasks that are usually considered part of project management?

7. Why is it important to consider Kahneman's fast and slow thinking in an Agile workspace, and what are your thoughts on the impact of biases in a leader's decision-making?
8. Why do you think mindfulness is beneficial in an agile work environment? Please comment on this statement "While primarily influencing slow thinking, mindfulness leads to a more balanced agile environment."

Chapter 6

Agile psychological development and CAMS

CHAPTER SUMMARY

The chapter explores the intricacies of balancing agile and planned approaches in work environments. The growing presence of agile psychology in the workplace requires maintaining a sense of equilibrium, embodied in the Composite Agile Method and Strategy (CAMS). The CAMS is a practical adaptation of agile in the workplace. This chapter further stresses the importance of psychological frameworks in achieving this balance, particularly through iterations and increments in agile. The concept of "fail-fast" is also delved into as a means of promptly identifying and addressing potential failures, which is the most effective approach to risk management.

INTRODUCTION

The existential reality of life is not straightforward and can often seem contradictory. This situation is also true of the modern workplace, which is quite complex. Agile as an approach to work does not fight against this complexity. Authentic agility, accompanied by its psychological understanding, takes a deep dive into the work's complexity and that of the worker. Successful leaders recognize that agility alone is not a solution to every workplace challenge. Instead, agile works much better when it is in harmony with planned approaches. Combining the strengths of Agile methodologies and planned approaches results in a balanced and effective way of working. This practical approach can benefit teams, organizations, and even entire societies.

The CAMS is a practical and balanced approach to work, achieved by combining the formality and governance of planned methods with the flexibility of Agile techniques. Successful leaders intuitively balance planned project management factors with Agile factors, leveraging their understanding of human nature. This chapter formalizes and discusses integrating Agile values and practices into an organization's formal methods. Leaders handle complexity by using iterations and increments to elicit feedback,

 DOI: 10.1201/9781003201540-6

incorporate changes, provide value, and reduce risks. CAMS combines agility and formal planning and control, architecture, design, and documentation, creating a balance that leads to success. The balancing in CAMS's applies across projects and organizations. However, successful implementation of CAMS requires a deep understanding of agile psychology. CAMS is not a static process set at the beginning of a project and followed through to completion. Instead, it adapts the Agile Manifesto in order to make it practical and adaptable through balance. Iterations and increments are crucial in Agile as they help reduce risks by identifying issues early on and understanding the value desired by clients. To achieve balance in practice, ongoing observations, facilitation, mentoring, and guidance from an agile leader are critical. The leader must understand technology, business needs, and team dynamics to balance human instincts, personalities, and aspirations with desired outcomes.

AGILE PSYCHOLOGY AND CAMS

Agile psychology keeps agility at the center of every action, based on collaboration, not competition. For this reason, it's important to consider how competition can negatively impact the future of Agile. While competition is inevitable, the Agile Manifesto and values transform competition from an individual's pursuit to a team sport. In an Agile environment, competition in the traditional sense doesn't work well and often contradicts the principles of agile. Good leaders understand the importance of collaboration over competition and strive to balance both. The traditional corporate culture of individuals working in silos to climb the hierarchical ladder is not conducive to Agile. The traditional levers for a manager using a "carrot and stick" approach are also not there to push in an agile environment. Changing this culture requires a shift in mindset for the team and the leader toward noncompetitive, unhurried, collaborative work.

This change in mindset toward a productive work environment integrates agile principles and practices with the existing ones from the planned approaches. The psychosocial foundation of CAMS is that agile should not merely react to the challenges posed by planned approaches but instead incorporate essential elements from planned approaches to ensure effective business organization. While the Agile Manifesto prioritizes "individuals and interactions over processes and tools," it's important to note that processes and tools support individuals in interacting and collaborating, especially in complex and extensive projects. For example, tools make developing and tracking a burndown chart in a real-life project possible. Therefore, promoting both individuals and their interactions with processes and tools is crucial. It can be challenging for some people to adjust to the iterative and Agile approach, especially if they are used to the more structured process of planning, modeling, and documentation. In such situations, leaders must be creative in ensuring team members understand the need to balance formal process-based lifecycles with agile methods. This requires considering factors such as psychology, sociology, and culture, which are even more crucial in such scenarios. Incorporating these factors into an organization's operations is a fundamental aspect of CAMS, differentiating it from exclusively Agile and entirely planned approaches.

CAMS incorporates the psychological factors of software development's complex and ambiguous nature. Often overlooked, the concept of "fuzziness" in processes is incorporated in CAMS. While the adage "we can't manage what we can't measure" has some truth, CAMS emphasizes the importance of non-measurable aspects of work. Leaders can accomplish many non-measurable pieces of work by applying the psychology of agile.

Agility's flexible nature presents challenges when estimating work without upfront and complete planning and design of the features. In Agile, incomplete or uncertain requirements are presented in user-story format on the Kanban board and discussed with the Product Owner and business stakeholders.[1] Work begins in an Agile project before the team fully understands the project's overall requirements because many requirements are explored as the solution development progresses. This situation creates a unique challenge that demands psychosocial understanding from the teams estimating work. Estimations in an Agile work environment become crucial as Agile teams often encounter unexpected technical challenges when they begin work. CAMS helps to understand the scope of the work and determine how long each task will take by breaking the features down into smaller tasks. This is called the work breakdown structure (WBS). Breaking a project into smaller iterations reduces the risk of delivering a complex product, as challenges or setbacks are limited to each iteration. This approach enables adjustments for subsequent iterations, mitigating risk and promoting adaptability. By making realistic estimates on a smaller piece of work, teams can make more accurate predictions of the time needed. Overestimating is preferable to underestimating as that helps the team account for unforeseen events.

CAMS supports planning and design to a certain level, with more intense analysis and design required in the first iteration of a multi-iteration project. The leader must continuously monitor and balance alterations in requirements, changes in underlying technologies, movement of personnel, and other related reasons. For example, removing a feature from an iteration due to a heavier workload is a delicate balancing act that involves all stakeholders who are integral to the decision-making process.

1 Unhelkar, B., *AI Adoption in Business Processes: The Agile Way*, Cutter Executive Update, Business Agility & Software Engineering Excellence Practice, Aug 2021, Vol. 22. No. 6, Cutter (an Arthur D. Little Company), Arlington, MA.

CAMS provides a holistic and balanced approach, which will most likely prevail as both a method and a strategy beyond software. A key reason for this prevalence is that CAMS acknowledges method friction and works to avoid it. Here are some principles of the CAMS approach:[2]:

- Planned approach for business, stakeholders, and solution requirements and Agile for development of the actual solution.
- Planned approach at the start of a project or any other business initiative that requires meticulous calculations of the costs, time, and scope of the initiative and Agile later in the project when the solution development commences.
- Planned approach on the client side of a project, wherein contracts still play an important role, and Agile on the vendor side (typically of an outsourced project) where the solution is being developed.
- Planned approach in the understanding of the problem and Agile in the delivery and deployment of the solution.
- Analytical on the problem side and synthetic on the solution side.
- Metric-based on the client/problem side and holistic on the solution side.
- Use of planned output during maintenance but Agile in exploring new development.

Agile values include trust, adaptability, empowerment, and collaboration. CAMS recognizes that every project is unique with its distinct requirements. Therefore, CAMS allows for a change of approach as work proceeds rather than following a predetermined route. Psychologically, CAMS develops a culture of sharing responsibilities, wherein team members think of the team's success rather than simply assigning tasks. Team members engage not only in their jobs but also in the overall aims of the iteration. As people work together toward a common goal, it strengthens team relationships. Developing trust among team members, creating a supportive atmosphere for joint problem-solving, sharing responsibilities, and celebrating accomplishments as a group leads to a cohesive work environment where planning, estimation, and architectural work of the first iteration can be carried out smoothly and creatively.

CAMS – A BALANCING ACT

The Linear, Waterfall, and Spiral lifecycles in the software world resulted from the need for formality and planning to reduce risks and prevent software disasters. The planning exercises and model creation provide estimates,

2 Unhelkar, B., 2013, *The Art of Agile Practice: A Composite Approach for Projects and Organizations*, CRC Press (Taylor and Francis Group/an Auerbach Book), Boca Raton, FL, USA.

controls, and guidance, while experienced programmers create patterns that designers use to develop high-quality solutions. In-depth requirement models also help users understand and provide input on expected outcomes. Despite these advantages, the human tendency to go to extremes often leads to projects becoming mired in excessive planning, documentation, and meetings on process compliance, with no visible output for the end-user. This is why Agile methodologies are increasingly popular. However, with the advent of Agile methodology, human tendencies to go to extremes shifted to the other side. The Agile Manifesto aimed to simplify the complex application of methods, resulting in some work environments with hardly any documentation. Scalability was also a hurdle in deploying Agile for larger projects, outsourced/off-shored development, large ERP (enterprise resource planning) configuration projects, and infrastructure projects requiring both agile and planned methods.

The key to unlocking the practical value of Agile is to maintain a balance between its principles. Additionally, it's beneficial to consider Agile's potential beyond software and in the broader realm of business solutions. The following is a revised view of the Agile Manifesto that strives for balance in a CAMS environment[3]:

- Individuals and interactions TOGETHER WITH processes and tools
- Working solution[4] TOGETHER WITH comprehensive documentation
- Customer collaboration TOGETHER WITH contract negotiation
- Responding to change TOGETHER WITH following a plan

This manifesto takes a fair and balanced approach by giving equal weight to both halves of each sentence. Maintaining this balance is the key to successfully implementing agility across the business-technology spectrum. CAMS is relevant at various organizational levels, from projects to departments, based on the relevant principles and practices. As a result, planned and Agile behaviors are integrated, and decisions are made considering the business, technology, and operational dimensions. CAMS promotes Agile practices throughout the organization with balance. CAMS is about balancing technology and business, formality and flexibility, and hierarchical and informal team structures. Emphasizing balance in this way is critical to the success of Agile implementation at all levels of the organization.

Psychologically, CAMS develops two key themes:

3 Unhelkar, B., 2012, *The Art of Agile Practice: A Composite Approach for Projects and Organizations*, Taylor and Francis/CRC Press, USA (Chapter 2).

4 While the original manifesto uses the word "software," the Disciplined Agile Manifesto talks about a solution (which may not be always a software one, especially if Agile is applied across the entire organization).

- *First, method:* Agile is a method that has excellent iteration and increment concepts – most notable being Scrum.[5] CAMS provides maximum value to projects when used in a composite mode that gives due deference to the existing methods in the organization. When applied in practice, the balance achieved by CAMS reduces method friction.
- *Second, strategy:* Agility at the organizational level is more than a method – it's an iterative and incremental business strategy. As a holistic strategy, CAMS permeates the entire organization, bringing about a culture change in the way of work. Such deployment of CAMS requires the organization's senior leadership to be actively involved in promoting and supporting agility.

CAMS streamlines collaboration across multiple work areas, such as User, Business, Project Management, Development, and Quality. CAMS creates a more cohesive and efficient work environment by minimizing friction between business processes, governance standards, project management, quality management, and business analysis. This is accomplished by striking the right balance between planning and agility at the outset of any initiative. CAMS adjusts this balance as the initiative progresses to ensure that both planned and agile elements work harmoniously, like a tightrope walker's balancing pole. With CAMS, leaders can seamlessly integrate planning and documentation with the collaborative nature of agile methodologies.

The CAMS approach encompasses a thorough understanding of the "soft" factors, which include socio-cultural and psychological elements, and incorporates them into an organizational strategy. For instance, coaching and training decision-makers in the organization ensure that strategy alignment, risk management, change management, and behavioral practices are in place, leading to greater agility.

CAMS combines scheduling, progress tracking, work assignment, and review with facilitation, roadblock removal, goal communication, and value provisioning. It places significant emphasis on creating opportunities for interaction, collaboration, dialogue, prototyping, and feedback. Furthermore, it nurtures questioning and listening skills.[6] Implementing Agile requires organizational changes such as dedicated team members and funding for coaching, training, and tools.

These changes, in turn, provide value and meet the expectations of users and stakeholders. Social interaction and cognitive skills play a crucial role in CAMS.[7]

5 Schwaber, K., and Beedle, M., 2001, *Agile Software Development with Scrum*, Prentice Hall, Upper Saddle River, NJ,

6 Unhelkar, B., *The Art of Questioning*, Cutter Executive Update, Vol. 15, No. 23, Business Technology Strategies Practice.

7 Lan, Y.-c., and Unhelkar, B., 2005, *Global Enterprise Transitions: Managing the Process*, IGI Global, Hershey, PA; Unhelkar, B., and Ginige, A., *A Framework to Derive Business Transformation Processes*, AeIMS Research Group, University of Western Sydney, 2009–2010.

The continuous balancing of work elements in CAMS provides the following business values:

- Customer experience is enhanced through immediate personalization of products and services. As the business interacts with customers, the ability to modify its offering instantly and maintain its compliance requirements is possible with CAMS.
- CAMS makes it easier for business partners to collaborate with the business because of the emphasis on balanced documentation, contracts, and compliance.
- Development of additional products and services is faster with input from analytics based on customer feedback.
- Enable a business to respond rapidly to sudden external changes (e.g., COVID-19) and the ensuing time-bound pressures to handle internal staff and external client needs.
- Reduce risks by initiating changes through strategic planning based on data-driven analytics to handle new technologies, regulatory changes, or market niches.
- Achieve technical flexibility with its IT systems that enable rapid changes and upgrades to the systems and provide extensibility through the Cloud.
- Facilitate increased collaboration with regulatory and compliance entities by extending the organization's reach within the region and globally.
- Enable ease of outsourcing and offshoring work based on the strength of the planned method's elements in the work environment.
- Facilitate lean-virtual business by reducing internal costs and improving the quality and efficiency of procurement, inventory, and development activities.
- Facilitate dynamicity in business processes by changing the organization's business processes to quickly and effectively respond to the customer's changing needs in a location- and time-independent manner.
- Ensure corporate responsibility by providing standards and consistency through governance frameworks. Improving corporate accountability and regulatory compliance through timely, accurate, and detailed reporting on business performance.
- Manage environmental responsibilities with lean and efficient business processes, efficient data centers, and sustainable HR policies.
- Enhance electronic presence through social media by exposing the right areas of the organization to customers, potential customers, and business partners.
- Enhance the user experience by enabling modeling and analyzing pre- and post-users in social media.[8]

8 Unhelkar, B., *User Experience Analysis Framework: From Usability to Social Media Networks,* Cutter Executive Report, April 2013, Vol. 13, No. 3, Data Insights and Social BI, Boston, USA.

CAMS emphasizes measuring progress through the use of tools that help identify the burndown progress, early detection of issues, promote visibility and, therefore, accountability, and facilitate effective stakeholder engagement. This measurable progress also offers valuable data for continuous improvement and is crucial for achieving success in Agile development.

Upskilling team members involves rotating roles within the organization. This rotation broadens their skills and enhances agility. For instance, a developer can gain valuable experience by temporarily taking on the role of a business analyst, acquiring skills such as interviewing stakeholders, documenting processes, and creating test cases.

The value of agile Retrospectives after each iteration cannot be overstated in boosting team capabilities. By facilitating reflection on the work process, this excellent psychosocial technique provides individuals and teams with valuable insights on making small, incremental improvements (also known as Kaizen) without assigning blame. As a group exercise, the retrospective encourages greater efficiency, quality, and collaboration in preparation for the next iteration.

CAMS prioritizes documenting the discussions and feedback, non-competitive reflection, and small, manageable improvements. Continuously accepting feedback, undertaking frequent product reviews, and adjusting the process results in an exemplary team. CAMS relies on the fact that the adaptability of an agile team is the result of psychosocial understanding rather than an enforced discipline.

PSYCHOLOGY OF ITERATIONS AND INCREMENTS IN CAMS

In an agile working environment, iterations and increments thoroughly explore requirements, develop a slice of the solution, display it, gather feedback, and then repeat the cycle in a slow, careful, and deliberate manner. The digital world is constantly evolving, and solutions that meet its requirements must be fluid and adaptable. The mindset of those involved in solution development is crucial. The iterative and incremental approach places equal emphasis on the process as well as the end product, focusing on flexibility and adaptability for swift adjustments in response to evolving requirements. CAMS extends this Agile work culture to include significant planning, estimation and design. During iteration planning, time and budget considerations are integrated with prioritizing critical and valuable work. Agile teams can adjust objectives and priorities based on changing needs, ensuring stakeholder value. By selecting user stories or tasks for the following iteration and prioritizing the most important ones, teams can easily respond to new information, user input, or business needs. This approach empowers teams to work nimbly and efficiently toward achieving their objectives.

The iterative work style in CAMS is also steadfastly committed to agile principles. For instance, while agile emphasizes flexibility, team members must still be dedicated to completing a specific set of tasks during each iteration. One of the most significant challenges in this process is the uncertainty or inaccuracy of estimations, which can lead to either overcommitment or underestimation of work.[9] The balance between task completion and avoiding overcommitment is achieved through CAMS. Pre-iteration planning and documentation, meticulous architectural and solution design in the first iteration, and a dedicated test strategy are all structured tasks in CAMS, which help the team understand their capabilities. As a result, undercommitment is avoided, and effective resource management is ensured. CAMS considers team capacity, task complexity, external dependencies, and process improvement to strike the perfect balance between adaptability and commitment. Successful CAMS iterations depend on well-balanced factors, resulting in a productive and satisfying work experience.

The CAMS iteration planning process is designed to use data from past iterations to develop velocity indicators that help guide the team's task commitments. It's crucial to strike a balance between flexibility and commitment, which is achieved through regular evaluations and feedback loops with stakeholders. To achieve this balance, assessing capacity, setting up buffers, prioritizing effectively, managing dependencies, and maintaining constant communication are all essential. Agile teams can navigate the challenges of planning and commitment by addressing these factors, producing valuable outcomes while remaining adaptable to shifting project dynamics. During iteration planning, team members work together to select and commit to user stories, promoting accountability and collaboration. By empowering team members to have a say in the project's planning and direction, they feel motivated and take ownership of their tasks with enthusiasm, resulting in sensible responsibilities and high-quality work during each iteration.

The CAMS approach enables teams to make incremental progress by delivering valuable product components to stakeholders early in the development of a solution. This approach also allows teams to respond quickly to changing market conditions and requirements. However, incomplete work from previous iterations can pose a challenge during iteration planning. To overcome this, teams should conduct comprehensive analyses of unfinished work during retrospectives and decide whether to progress tasks to the next iteration or eliminate them from future iterations. Additionally, team leaders often use the CAMS approach to under-promise and overdeliver.

Effective decision-making relies heavily on open communication among team members, particularly when it comes to accurately estimating user

9 For more discussions, see Cohn, M., 2005, *Agile Estimating and Planning*, Prentice Hall, Upper Saddle River, NJ.

stories or backlog items. One practical way to overcome this challenge is to involve everyone and refer to previous iterations. This method aligns with the principles of continuous improvement, which are closely tied to iterations and increments. The use of a Kanban board offers a visual representation of the workflow and allows for ongoing evaluation and improvement. The philosophy of Kaizen, which emphasizes continuous improvement, is closely linked to Kanban. Furthermore, teams should engage in a retrospective after each iteration, which is a crucial agile practice that fosters a culture of learning and development. The Kanban board is a valuable tool for tracking tasks, monitoring their progress, and identifying potential roadblocks. Additionally, Kanban extends beyond the team's internal operations and involves communication with external stakeholders..

ADVANTAGES OF ITERATIVE APPROACH

The benefits of the iterative way of work, including the iteration planning process, are clear and yet warrant further discussion. Iterations offer numerous advantages over a linear approach, such as the ability to adapt to changing requirements and swiftly respond to emerging issues. With digitization being an integral part of practically every business process, data-driven decision-making has mandated the need for an iterative and incremental approach to work. Breaking work into smaller pieces and handling them one at a time allows for continuous progress monitoring, promoting a culture of learning and adaptation that ultimately leads to higher-quality products and more efficient processes. CAMS places great emphasis on detailed planning for each iteration, taking into account time and budget constraints. By prioritizing the most important user stories while considering these constraints, teams enjoy the flexibility, adaptability, alignment, and risk reduction benefits of iterative planning. Flexibility allows teams to accommodate sudden new requirements, while adaptability enables changes to plans as needed. Iteration planning also improves the visibility of work, enabling stakeholders to see progress and express approval or request changes much sooner than in a non-iterative approach. Alignment is critical to ensure that development work satisfies specified requirements, while risk reduction is achieved through the "fail-fast" mechanism. Conducting retrospectives after each iteration further improves the benefits of this approach, facilitating the learning process and leading to better quality control and decision-making.

CHALLENGES OF ITERATIVE APPROACH

The iterative approach to work can be challenging, particularly when it comes to task estimation and balancing time and scope. This challenge is especially pronounced when working with uncharted technologies or fields and inexperienced teams. Accurately gauging the time and effort required for each task can prove difficult. However, team members can improve their estimations by discussing potential obstacles, exchanging viewpoints, and collaborating to develop realistic estimates. Teams should prioritize tasks based on business value and complexity while also considering their capacity and historical velocity. Overcommitting can lead to fatigue and missed deadlines, while under-committing can cause inefficiencies and slow progress. The team can overcome this challenge by utilizing historical data and their previous velocity as the basis for their forecasts. Estimations of the entire project can improve with total participation from all team members. However, whether it's "due to the pressure to conform, pressure to present themselves in a favorable way... shyness and poor team spirit",[10] problems with team participation can lead to insufficient or incorrect estimations in the iteration planning phase. It's essential to be realistic about what can be accomplished and to under-commit rather than overpromise. Prioritizing the importance and difficulty of user stories or tasks can also ensure that only the most critical and feasible elements are included in the iteration. Regular retrospectives can facilitate continual improvement in estimation and capacity management over time.

In the fast-paced digital world, priorities can shift suddenly and dramatically. Customer preferences, regulations, and cybersecurity risks constantly evolve, and events like the COVID-19 pandemic add to the complexity and uncertainty. This can make planning challenging and lead to conflicting demands, changes to the plan, and impacts on timelines and stakeholder satisfaction. To navigate this landscape, engaging in regular dialogue with stakeholders and prioritizing based on business value is critical. During planning sessions, reviewing and revising priorities based on the latest information is important and documenting all changes for post-iteration evaluations is important. Also, establishing a change management procedure requiring approval for new scope requests can prevent hastily implemented changes.

Managing dependencies between different parts of a project can be difficult when working iteratively. This is especially true when one aspect of the product relies on another that hasn't been developed yet. Dependencies can be especially challenging when it comes to non-functional requirements like performance, scalability, and cybersecurity, making them a major obstacle during iterations. To address this, CAMS takes on significant planning and architectural work during the initial iteration, identifying major dependencies on non-functional requirements and planning for frequent showcasing of the product under development. Continuous integration of product slices and ongoing testing is also key to handling dependency challenges and

10 Drury, Conboy, K., and Power, K., "Obstacles to Decision Making in Agile Software Development Teams," *The Journal of Systems and Software*, 2012, 85(6), 1239–1254. https://doi.org/10.1016/j.jss.2012.01.058

ensuring seamless product releases with minimal integration issues. CAMS also creates a roadmap for the work before the first iteration to reduce uncertainty and mitigate risks.

Scope creep can pose a challenge in the iterative approach, as discussed in Chapter 4, the Flour Mix game. To mitigate this, CAMS recommends consistent communication with stakeholders and implementing a thorough change management process from the beginning. While this process may seem bureaucratic, it is crucial in avoiding scope creep. New requests or changes to existing requirements undergo a streamlined procedure that assesses their impact on the current iteration.

RISK MANAGEMENT IN CAMS – A FAIL-FAST APPROACH

Effective risk management is essential in an agile work environment, and adopting an iterative and incremental approach is crucial to achieving this. By dividing a project into well-planned, small iterations, identifying and assessing risks at an early stage becomes feasible. This is because any issues or flaws within the project become clear during the initial iteration. The CAMS principle of risk management emphasizes the importance of recognizing potential obstacles and hazards, and making regular adjustments throughout iterations to mitigate risks effectively, even if they are not significant.

Establishing a strong partnership with business stakeholders is essential to minimize risk in CAMS. It is important to gather regular feedback from stakeholders from the outset of the project to reduce risk. While technology risks are a concern, the greater risk lies in producing a product that does not meet the desired business outcomes. Stakeholder feedback based on an upfront prototype and working product helps in managing the risk. While conceptual ideas are valuable, they do not provide direct input for improving a digital product. Maintaining a continuous feedback loop is vital in avoiding misunderstandings and misaligned expectations, resulting in higher-quality output and fewer surprises. Agile iteration planning offers flexibility to adjust work items as risks arise, allowing for proactive risk management throughout the project's lifecycle.

By developing the solution iteratively, the initial stages provide valuable insights into whether the product is headed in the right direction. Moreover, early iterations can help identify and resolve minor technical glitches. Embracing the bold approach of failing sooner rather than later is essential to risk management in CAMS. This approach recognizes that overlooking potential risks is a common challenge. While it's critical to prioritize feature delivery and meet stakeholder demands, it's equally important to dedicate sufficient time and attention to detailed risk assessment and mitigation planning. Teams must consider technical dependencies and business changes continually to strike a balance between delivering items and managing risks.

This process involves discovering new requirements, identifying relevant technologies, and aligning the solution output with business outcomes to mitigate risks effectively.

CONSOLIDATION WORKSHOP

1. How does CAMS integrate planned and Agile aspects of work? Identify one activity from the planned, linear approach and another from the agile approach that can be carried out jointly.
2. In CAMS, why is a shift in mindset crucial? How does understanding the psychology of Agile aid in adopting the CAMS mindset? *(Hint: CAMS is all about balance between planned and agile.)*
3. What are your thoughts on the modified Agile Manifesto? Can you provide practical examples to support your discussion?
4. What would you consider as the key psychological theme of CAMS?
5. How do CAMS iterations and increments translate into practical work? What are the benefits and challenges of an iterative approach to work?
6. What is the concept of "fail-fast," and how can it be applied to risk management in CAMS?
7. How does CAMS foster continuous learning, considering the principles of Kaizen and Kanban?

Chapter 7

Agile organizational structures and behaviors

CHAPTER SUMMARY

This chapter discusses the impact of adopting an Agile methodology on group structure and behavior. It emphasizes the importance of considering the psycho-social aspects of group culture and how they influence team dynamics. Agile culture is collaborative, flatter, informal, encourages engagement and is participative. Understanding each team member's unique perspectives and motivations can create a productive and enjoyable group culture with its agile structures and dynamics. The chapter also extends the "I" concept discussed in earlier chapters and how it shapes the team and the organization. Agile organizational structure is a responsive work environment. The chapter further emphasizes CAMS's balanced planned and Agile structures to ensure adaptability, leading to greater efficiency and better outcomes.

INTRODUCTION

Collaboration and responsiveness are integral to the Agile approach which has a non-hierarchical, informal team structure. Group structure and dynamics are impacted by individual perspectives and motivations that shape behavior. Building on the importance of balance discussed earlier, this chapter details how agile organizational structures are grounded in the CAMS framework. This chapter further underscores that Agile teams are self-organizing and work toward a common goal. Therefore, in Agile teams, group dynamics assume utmost importance. How a group is structured is fundamental to effective group dynamics. Agile emphasizes the team and its culture; therefore, the structure and dynamics of agile teams will have a culture that fosters open communication, shares ideas and provides non-threatening feedback. Trust in teams is built through transparency and accountability. Agile team structures are based on a strong commitment to teamwork and a willingness to work collaboratively.

DOI: 10.1201/9781003201540-7

AGILE ORGANIZATIONAL STRUCTURES

Organizational structures refer to how a group of individuals is arranged or organized. The roles, responsibilities, reporting lines, and entry-exit points define the structure. Essentially, organizational structures are how people are put together in the workplace. Agile organizational structures are popular due to their adaptability and flexibility. There are three widely recognized types of organizational structures: functional, product-based, and matrix. These structures can be either hierarchical (pyramid) or Agile (flattened) within each type. Each structure has its unique benefits and drawbacks, so deciding which to implement depends on the organization's specific needs.

- The functional structure is a traditional organizational model based on specific functions or departments. It is most effective in organizations with well-defined roles and a clear hierarchy. However, the functional structure has a siloed effect, making cross-departmental collaboration challenging. Thus, it will not be able to handle the cross-functional teams prevalent in agile approaches.
- The product-based structure is designed to support the development of new products or services. It necessitates cross-functional teams for each project, resulting in a more collaborative work environment. However, this structure may lack oversight and coordination across the organization.
- The matrix structure combines cross-functional teams while maintaining a hierarchical structure. It is ideal for organizations that require both efficiency and flexibility. However, it can lead to conflict among team members due to competing priorities and unclear decision-making processes.

CAMS agile structures balance flexibility with the rigors of planning and tracking. Agile structures are implemented at various levels within a company, such as small teams, departments, divisions, and the entire organization. The success of an agile structure depends on finding a balance between these levels while aligning with the company's culture and objectives. A team's ability to adapt to changing circumstances and collaborate toward a common goal by empowering each member's unique strengths and viewpoints is essential. CAMS considers the unique needs and capabilities of the team, ensures a balanced structure, and fosters a culture of continuous improvement. Analytical methods are generally preferred in planned and hierarchical organizational structures, whereas agile strategies tend to produce holistic and non-hierarchical structures. Although departments and divisions still exist in agile organizations, they serve different functions in this balanced, mixed organization type. Every action is focused on providing value to the end user, and leadership takes precedence over management in a CAMS workplace culture.

GROUP DYNAMICS IN AGILE

The Agile Manifesto's first statement emphasizes individuals and their interactions. Positive interaction among individuals advances the group's shared objective. However, humans are naturally territorial and tend to hold onto their physical and mental boundaries. Collaboration challenges this territorial mindset and makes boundaries more permeable. The most challenging aspect of agile culture change is for individuals to accept and comprehend the need to break down these territorial barriers. Collaboration depends on understanding how two (or more) individuals interact and relate to each other continuously. Developing this understanding requires a study of the transactions that occur on an ongoing basis between two individuals, multiple individuals within teams, multiple teams within the organization, and later between organizations and society. The mechanism of transactions was discussed in detail in Chapter 4, transactional analysis (TA).

Individuals and groups

Figure 7.1 summarizes various factors influencing individuals and groups and how they map to Maslow's hierarchy at different levels. The primary focus is on fulfilling physiological and safety needs at the individual level while emphasizing Agile tools and techniques. The next level is that of a group, where individuals come together and collaborate to create a sense of belongingness and support. This helps to build Agile team structures based on collaboration and belongingness. The overall business organization,

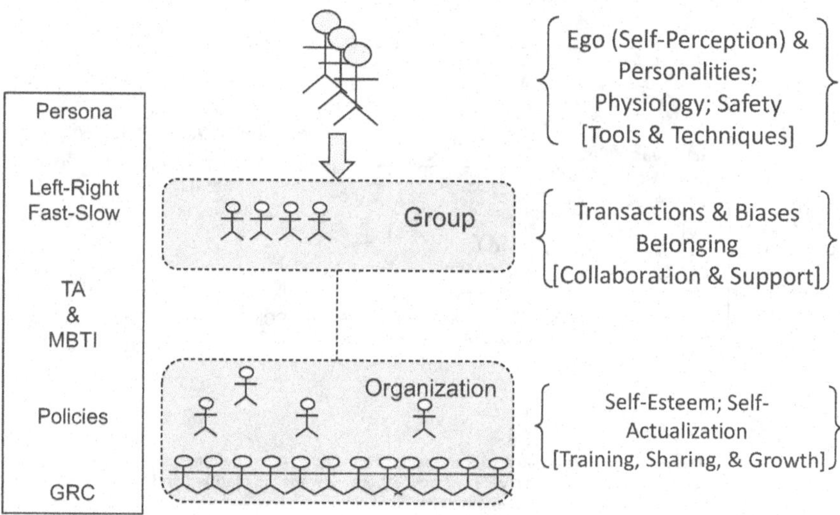

Figure 7.1 From Individual to Groups to Organization.

comprising multiple groups, their personalities, and transactions, can create a work environment where individuals can achieve complete fulfillment, and self-esteem can reach its peak. Figure 7.1 also serves as a reminder of the psycho-social frameworks used in creating and managing groups.

The "I" and "my view" in a group

Individuals form a group. However, an even more appropriate description would be that an individual's view of himself and that of another of themselves form a group. An agile team, which is a group, thus comprises individuals' views of themselves and fellow team members. These views may differ from how a person in reality fits into a group. An individual's view of themselves may prevent them from expressing their opinions or countering others' opinions of themselves. Other team members also perceive an individual based on their views of the individual and themselves. This situation develops out of the "Johari's window" discussed in an earlier chapter. Figure 7.2 shows three circles representing (a) the real "I," (b) my view of "I," and (c) my view of "how others view me." In these circles, the real "I" results from the Adult ego state. The two "views" circles operating out of the Parent ego state create stereotypes, which are strongly held beliefs by a person – about themselves and others. Stereotypes lead to biases in a person's perception that often confirm their expectations about others irrespective of authenticity. This situation may result in conflicts and disagreements due to cultural differences and stereotypes. It is crucial to be aware of these

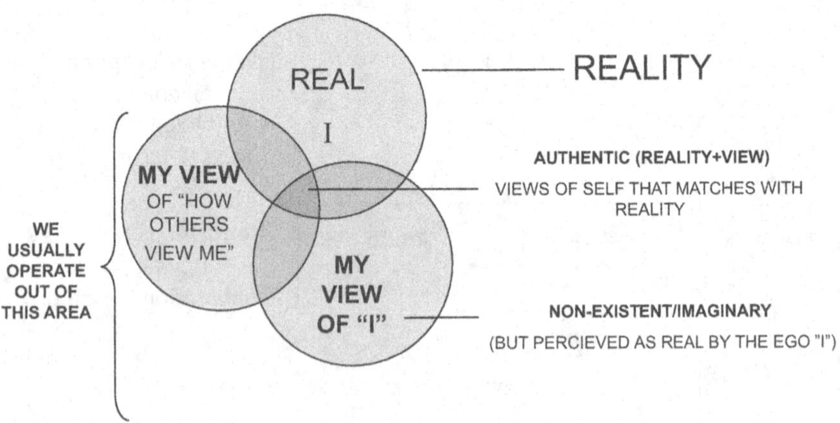

Figure 7.2 Individual's "I" View as Basis for Formation of Groups.

stereotypes, even if team members come from similar cultural backgrounds, to ensure the smooth functioning of an Agile group. These smooth group dynamics and open communication are essential for effective collaboration. The biggest challenge for a leader is to bridge the gap between the actual and perceived views of team members toward each other.

Distorted "my view" leads to team friction

Berne, in his book *Structure and Dynamics of Organizations and Groups*, outlines the impact of stereotypes and perceptions on a group.[1] Stereotypical behavior is based on a distorted view that a person has about where and how they fit into a group. Separating "my view" of myself and the actual "I" is essential for understanding group behavior. Figure 7.3 demonstrates this distorted view. On the left in Figure 7.3 is a typical agile team with seven members. There is one coach or facilitator (typically a Scrum Master). A team member in discussion is one of the remaining six members who do not work in any hierarchy. This agile team is collaborative and cross-functional, with each team member bringing expertise to the work. If the team member in discussion operates outside his or her Adult ego state, they will perceive themselves differently. In Figure 7.3, the image on the

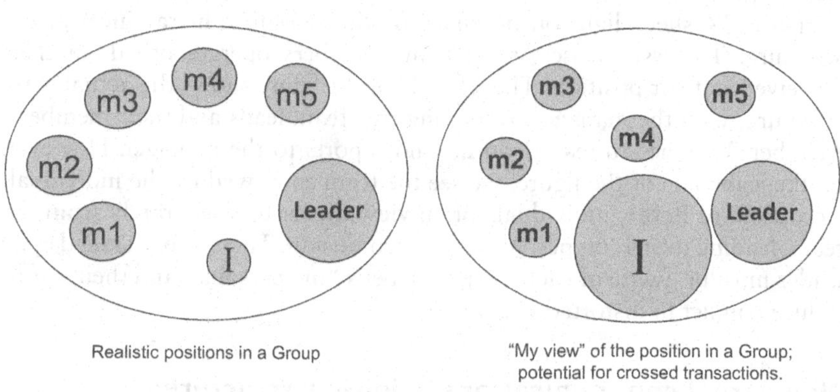

Figure 7.3 Individuals in Agile Groups Need To Be Aware of Their Potentially Distorted View of the Group Structure as There Is Much Less Rigor in terms of the Hierarchy.

1 Berne, E. (1963). *Structure and dynamics of organizations and groups*, Ballantine Books, New York, p. 19, Figure 7 A and B for those interested.

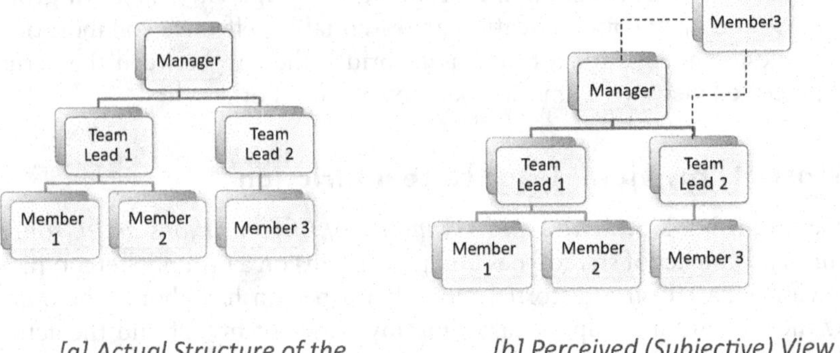

Figure 7.4 Example of an Actual Structure and Perceived Structure Based on "My View" of an Individual in a Team.

right portrays a distorted and exaggerated view of oneself, which is the as a stereotype. This skewed perception can lead to tension and conflict among team members, particularly if others are also grappling with their stereotypes.

Figure 7.4 sheds light on potential friction within a hierarchical group structure. The issue arises when team members operate based on their perceived state or position. The left side of the figure shows the actual team structure, with the manager overseeing two team leads and their members. Member 3 reports to team lead 2, who reports to the manager. However, on the right side of the figure, we see the team as viewed by the individual. According to Berne, individuals often view themselves separately from the team, leading to stereotypes, biases, and confusion. Therefore, a skilled agile leader must be aware of each team member's "my persona" and their self to reduce conflict in distorted situations.

Non-verbal communications in loosely structured agile teams

Incorporating agility into a team greatly enhances non-verbal communication and vice versa. An agile team is structured in an informal manner with multiple dotted lines for reporting and with the leader serving as a facilitator rather than a director. In the Scrum framework, the Scrum Master is officially called the "Servant-Leader." In such a setting, perceiving oneself, others and how others perceive us becomes crucial as a basis for all

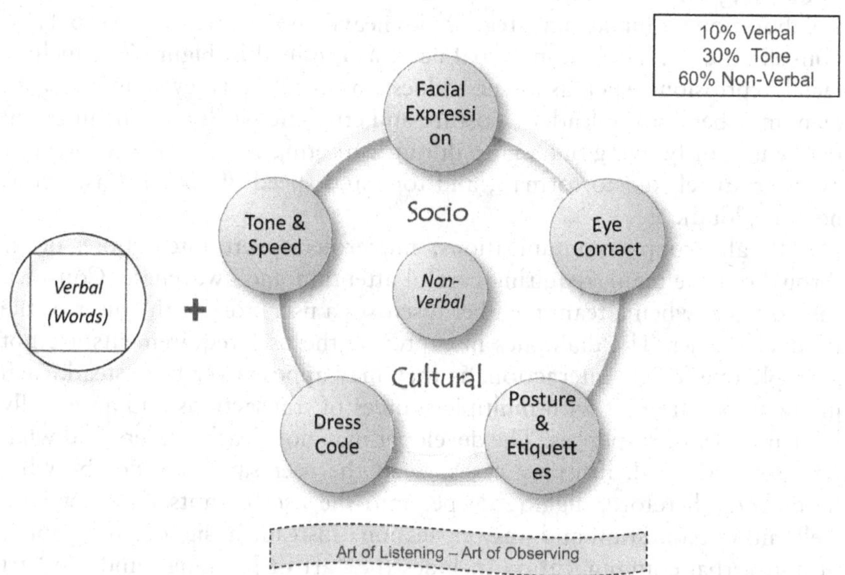

Figure 7.5 **Paying Extra Attention to Non-Verbal Communication with the Art of Listening and the Art of Observing with a Functioning Adult Provides Opportunities for Complimentary Transactions.**

communication. According to Mehrabian (1981),[2] non-verbal communication, including body language and tone of voice, makes up 90% of the emotional message conveyed in communication. Agile ceremonies such as daily stand-ups, showcasing, and retrospectives are situations where non-verbal communication is far more important than words.

Being respectfully aware of "my view" and paying extra attention to how non-verbal communication occurs in agile teams can help alleviate the many team issues and challenges that impact agile work environments. Awareness of "views" helps develop an Adult ego state-based communication that includes words, voice, and body language. While Mehrabian's body-language research states that 55% of communication is non-verbal, 38% is vocal, and 7% is words only, Figure 7.5 provides an indicative set of numbers highlighting the tremendous importance of non-verbal communication.

Group dynamics with agile teams are already complex due to individuals' innumerable biases and multitude of personas – none of which are the "real self." The fact that non-verbal communication carries a large percentage

2 Mehrabian, A., 1981, *Silent Messages: Implicit Communication of Emotions and Attitudes* (2nd ed.), Wadsworth, Belmont, CA, USA, ISBN 0-534-00910-7.

of meaning can result in heavily skewed interactions and friction. Effective collaboration within an agile team relies heavily on awareness of verbal and non-verbal cues. These non-verbal cues, as outlined in Figure 7.5, include facial expressions (such as anger, sadness, or disinterest), eye contact (with team members or the leader), posture and etiquette (such as slouching, cell phone use, or blowing one's nose during a meeting), dress code (which can range from relaxed to formal), and tone and speed of speech (fast, slow, nervous, loud).

With all group communications, numerous covert interactions occur throughout the team, requiring careful attention and awareness. Consider, for example, when a team member discusses a user story with a user or the Product Owner. The dialogues in capturing the user requirements are not a simple one-to-one interaction, as they may appear overtly. Instead, each interaction is fraught with multiple sources of transactions and an equally large number of responses. The developer may not clearly understand what the user says, and, in many cases, what the user says may not be what he meant. Therefore, digging deeper into the user's wants may not be a well-laid-out question-and-answer session. Instead, a significant amount of non-verbal communication includes the "art of listening" and the "art of observation," as illustrated in Figure 7.5. Failing to recognize these non-verbal cues can result in misunderstandings and misinterpretations of communications.

Furthermore, when an entire organization adopts an Agile approach, the complexity of interactions between individuals and between teams is multiplied. Various psycho-social factors become crucial in these situations beyond agile techniques and protocols. For instance, social skills, group acceptance, political maneuvering, and psychological fears and concerns come into play when adopting and utilizing agile approaches. Non-verbal communications recognize that a person's ego states from where he or she communicates are not static but continuously change, providing a window for individual expression.

Organizational adoption of agile requires recognition of these ego states. Creating opportunities for the expression of these ego states and, at times, even their suppression is a vital part of the psychosociology of agile. In a daily stand-up meeting, for example, team members can be encouraged to suspend their Child tendencies and instead focus on aligning with the team goals through their functioning Adult personality. On the other hand, one can see the importance of social events, such as the coffee machine or the after-hour drinks, where the child personality of an individual has an opportunity to express itself. Incorporation of humor and laughter is highly encouraged and deemed essential in an agile organization because it is the need of the inner child within each individual.

Emotions expressed by the Child ego state effectively releases stress and fosters a positive and enjoyable work environment. Embracing and encouraging humor and laughter also creates a sense of unity amongst team members. While individuals are the building blocks of a team, the team also influences each individual's mindset. Together, individuals and teams create an organization's overall character. This character is communicated non-verbally, regardless of marketing, advertisement, and sales efforts. The non-verbal character of a group, whether it's a small agile team or an entire agile organization, is its gestalt.

AIDING AGILE TEAM STRUCTURES AND BEHAVIORS

The composite agile approach has various built-in supports that benefit an agile team's structure and behavior. This section highlights some of these supports, which can considerably reduce team friction and improve agile team performance. These supports include coaching and mentoring, inspection and adaptation, reflection and retrospectives, and agile job aids for its practices.

Coaching and mentoring

Coaching and mentoring team members is an ongoing activity that an agile leader undertakes. Coaching team members to apply a psycho-social framework of their choice in interacting with one another can help reduce crossed transactions and unnecessary interference in group dynamics. Agile coaching is in social behavior, the use of agile practices, and Agile adoption. Mentoring is closely associated with coaching and deals with the leader's follow-up actions. An external coach is far more valuable in agile transformation, bringing impartial and unbiased knowledge and agility experience to help the team apply agile techniques. A trusted coach can also help resolve many political and territorial issues within groups by being an outsider and, therefore, not aligned with a particular faction. Cross-cultural disparities are also smoothed out by coaching and mentoring. When multiple cultures have to work together on a project, the high- and low-context discussion in Chapter 3 becomes relevant. These disparities become prominent in outsourced projects where people from two or more widely varying cultural backgrounds must work together. For example, Japanese culture encourages the experience of socially engaging emotions (e.g., friendly feelings, sympathy, and guilt), whereas Western culture encourages socially disengaging emotions (e.g., pride and territory). Coaching team members to be aware of cross-cultural disparities and mentoring them when they embark on new initiatives is most helpful in agile adoption.

When a senior leader is present within a group that it transforming to agile, it can significantly alter the group dynamic, sending a non-verbal signal that change is being embraced from the top. This is especially crucial when adopting the agile mindset, as agile is more of a cultural change than a technical one. In-house training and coaching sessions can benefit significantly from having the highest-ranking leader address the individuals, even if it's just for a few minutes, to emphasize the importance of agility in their business strategy.

Inspection and adaptation

A key tenet of Agile thinking is "inspect and adapt." Continuous inspection and adaptation are not limited to product development. Numerous business processes (both customer-facing and internal) benefit immensely from inspection and adaptation. The agile team structure and team leadership can thrive on the culture of inspection of processes and adaptation to the changing context in which the processes are operating. For example, the well-known use case "customer withdraws cash" can be changed in many different ways to adapt to the customer's location, desired amount, and urgency. Continuous inspection and adaptation increase the team's value in the way it operates and higher value to the end user. Adapting to newer agile practices requires a change of mindset, and a good agile leader will make provision for the inculcation of that new mindset in every team activity.

Reflection and retrospectives

Reflection is essential for establishing and maintaining an effective agile team. It is crucial to reflect on how the cross-functional team was assembled and operated during each iteration to establish a productive team structure and behavior. This reflective characteristic is well integrated into the agile practice of retrospectives, which the team carries out at the end of a specific project. Nevertheless, even when the team is not involved in project work, it is still valuable to conduct retrospectives to identify which aspects of daily operations are functioning well and which areas require improvement to contribute to the organization's success. Since agile methodology emphasizes supportive teamwork, honest reflection is a foundation for personal performance enhancement and innovative growth.

Retrospectives serve as a valuable tool for teams to reflect internally, but in a CAMS-based working environment, external observers may also play a role. This is especially beneficial in Agile workplaces that extend beyond project-oriented work, as external perspectives from fields like humanities can enhance the team's overall work experience. Additionally, this practice can be expanded to include identifying team members' key performance indicators (KPIs) from an HR standpoint. While modern Agile practices may not prioritize traditional HR-monitored performance reviews that lead to promotions and bonuses, these elements remain crucial motivators. One potential solution is incorporating team-based events, similar to retrospectives, to evaluate performance and rewards. Embracing a team-based rewarding structure can greatly benefit Agile workplaces. When performance of individuals within a group is assessed, the leader must be aware of the biases and personalities within the group. Individuals' decisions are often influenced by the perceived value of their work, their perceived position in the group, and the impact of biases on their estimation and prioritization. Therefore, careful monitoring of these factors is necessary to ensure fair evaluations.

Agile job aids for practices

Agile teams integrate Agile practices into their daily work. Chapter 2's Figure 2.4 outlines helpful Agile job aids that can facilitate adoption. As teams transition to Agile, they can continue to coach, inspect, and reflect while experimenting with one job aid at a time. This method of learning the agile practices aligns with the Agile concept of iterations and increments. Rotating the job aids enables team members to become proficient in these practices. It may take approximately three months of daily use of these job aids to reach full proficiency. As proficiency increases, the aids become less necessary. During the Agile adoption process, these Job Aids can be printed and displayed on an Agile wall for easy reference.

PLANNED VERSUS AGILE GROUP STRUCTURES AND DYNAMICS

Figure 7.6 compares the structure and dynamics of groups based on planned and Agile approaches. This comparison is essential to understand the functioning of an Agile culture in the teams. This comparison can also be related to the team structures based on TA life positions discussed in Chapter 4.

The top portion of Figure 7.6 illustrates a planned approach, which employs a hierarchical group structure with precise boundaries. These structures have historically proven effective in manufacturing and construction industries. Some teams, such as legal and accounting firms, are inherently rigid due to their organizational function. In these teams, directives come from the top down, and an individual's position or role carries more weight than their contributions to the team's overall performance. Task management and metrics dominate the team culture, leaving little room for individual creativity. In contrast with the limitations on creativity, these structures and dynamics offer stability necessary for these functions.

In Figure 7.6, the lower two squares illustrate the structures and dynamics of Agile teams. Agile groups have a flat, egalitarian organizational structure, with cross-functional teams and flexible boundaries centered around self-motivated individuals. This results in porous and fluid team dynamics that promotes collaborative work. The Agile teams function differently to

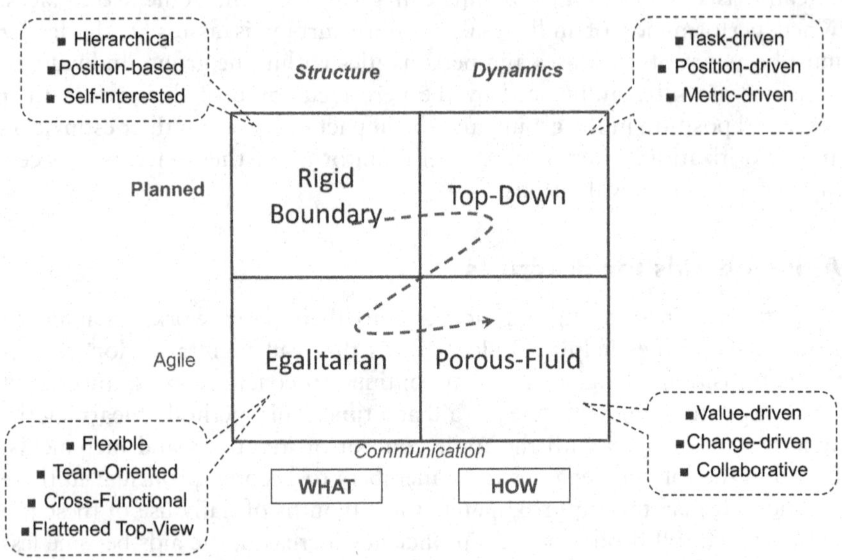

Figure 7.6 Planned versus Agile Group Structures and Dynamics.

traditionally organized teams. As a result, even the concept of "communication" takes on different meanings in Agile, as discussed earlier with non-verbal communication.

In their reengineering approach to business, Michael Hammer and James Champy explored "flattening the pyramid of the organizational structure."[3] This idea is relevant to Agile team structures as well. A synchronous CAMS team operates without a hierarchical pyramid structure, opting for a relatively flat organization instead. Such a structure fosters a less rigid reporting system and encourages hands-off leadership. This approach ultimately leads to greater value, as team members can synchronize their efforts when they possess a clear understanding of shared values, direction, and risks.

Figure 7.7 depicts how a CAMS team blends planned and agile elements. The iron triangle of project management, which includes time, cost, and scope, is based on the traditional Waterfall-driven approach. On the other hand, the agile aspects of a CAMS project contribute to qualities like value and constraints. While stakeholders' interests may overlap, the user/sponsor of the project is typically concerned with value, the developer/manager with quality, and the business architect/regulator with constraints. Ultimately, a CAMS team is a well-structured blend of planned and agile elements, which combines a linear approach with iterations and increments.

3 Hammer, M., and Champy, J., 2001, *Reengineering the Corporation: A Manifesto for Business Revolution* (3rd ed.), Nicholas Brealey Publishing, London, UK.

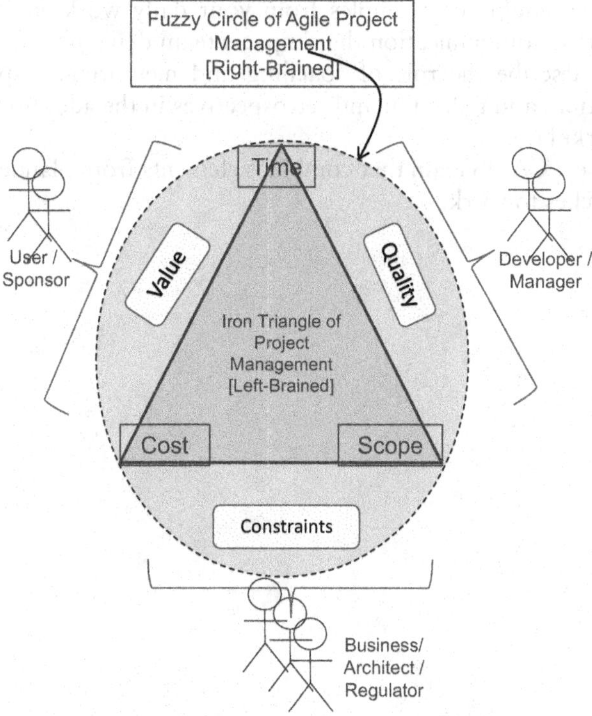

Figure 7.7 Stakeholders in Agile Groups (Merging Planned and Agile Approaches in Practice Creates Opportunities for Different Stakeholders to Work Together).

CONSOLIDATION WORKSHOP

1. Why is it important for Agile teams and organizational structures to be flatter? Explain why a hierarchical organizational structure will not enable an agile work environment.
2. What are the key differences between the group structures of planned and agile teams? List an advantage and a challenge of each.
3. How can a leader circumvent the challenge of distorted personas and ensure that "my view" of the role of an individual does not distort the team structure?
4. How does a distorted view of an individual team member prevent genuine interactions between two or more individuals? What can be done to reduce this distortion?
5. How does an individual shape the personality of a team? What role can a leader play in ensuring a positive, agile work culture through understanding biases and personas?

6. Why is non-verbal communication important, especially in agile teams? Provide a couple of examples from your daily work environment of non-verbal communication that impacts team dynamics.
7. Briefly describe the role of coaching and mentoring, inspection and adaptation, and reflection and retrospectives in the adoption of agile in the workplace.
8. Describe a CAMS team that combines elements from planned and agile approaches to work.

Chapter 8

Agile transformations in the digital age

CHAPTER SUMMARY

In today's digital era psychology of agile is set to play a crucial role. In order to be relevant to clients, organizations must have the ability to respond quickly, be proactive, and be forward-thinking. This chapter delves into the relationship between agile transformations and the digital landscape, exploring how data science, including data analytics and Artificial Intelligence, can assist in the transition to organizational agility. Additionally, the chapter highlights key psychosocial traits that are necessary for a successful agile transformation, as well as modern digital leadership qualities that are essential for creating an agile organization.

INTRODUCTION

Agility is closely connected to the digital age. The rapid evolution of Artificial Intelligence, Big Data, cybersecurity, and communication networks has transformed how organizations are structured and operate.[1] Agile is appropriate as an organizational structure for the digital age, but it requires leaders to be innovative. The Agile Manifesto, which values change and encourages responding to change rather than sticking to a plan, supports this idea. Leaders in an agile organization respond to change and utilize digital technologies to welcome unplanned change and unforeseen outcomes. This is why there is a need for substantial innovativeness in applying digital capabilities in business. The outcomes produced by digitalization need to be integrated into the mosaic of Agile corporate goals.[2] An Agile organization can promptly and effectively respond to internal and external changes. It is a collaborative, interconnected, and communicative entity that operates

1 Unhelkar, B., and Gonsalves, T., 2021, *Artificial Intelligence for Business Optimization*, Routledge (Taylor and Francis Group), USA.

2 Tiwary, A., and Unhelkar, B., 2018, *Outcome-Driven Business Architecture*, CRC Press (Taylor and Francis Group/an Auerbach Book), Boca Raton, FL, USA.

DOI: 10.1201/9781003201540-8

harmoniously with the surrounding ecosystem, including industry, government, and society. Transforming into an Agile organization requires a shift from being slow-moving, inefficient, rigid, hierarchical, and disconnected from the environment to being aligned with the dynamic external world and fully engaged with customers and partners. The agility of such an organization results from holistically harnessing the capabilities of digital technologies, embedding data-driven decision-making in its business processes, implementing robust processes around cybersecurity and privacy, and ensuring anticipatory risk management. This chapter discusses the concepts behind such a holistic organization, the multilayered nature of agility, the importance of handling paradox, and the value of non-competitiveness in generating significance beyond success.

AGILE TRANSFORMATIONS

Shifting an organization's culture from task management to a more collaborative and facilitative work style is a significant undertaking. It requires a shift in mindset that can only be achieved by delving into people's core motivations, analyzing interactions between individuals, and identifying underlying biases in decision-making. The coach's role in this transformation is to enable the team to operate at its highest level while protecting it from external influences and eliminating possible roadblocks. Agile is an attractive framework for achieving this, but its adoption can be disruptive as it challenges established working methods. Practical challenges come with implementing Agile, including ambiguity around the term itself. Agile can be interpreted differently depending on the individual and context. Developers often see it as a methodology for delivering solutions, while business leaders are drawn to its promise of faster delivery and increased business value. To successfully transform an organization with Agile, it is necessary to have a comprehensive understanding and application of it at all levels.

Changes occur at various organizational levels that transform into an agile culture. Work carried out in an Agile transformation also elevates the Agile coaching and mentoring concepts from projects to organizational functioning. The holistic working style for an organization is a significant change in mindset. Due to reduced friction, agile organizations require far less effort in projects and operations than non-agile organizations. When a team gels, it experiences minimal friction and maximum output. Leadership during Agile transformations at an organizational level needs to be fully aware of their assumptions and biases. Such a change in working style requires demonstrated support and direction from leaders. Active participation from leadership on an ongoing basis is integrated into an Agile transformation.

DIGITAL BUSINESS

At the organizational level, agility prioritizes flexibility and collaboration over hierarchy and planning. This approach allows for swift responsiveness to changing business needs. Achieving this level of agility is not the responsibility of just one internal team. The responsibility for agility extends to the entire organization, including external entities such as customers, business partners, and regulatory agencies.[3] In today's digital market, an organization needs to continuously review and update its technological and infrastructural frameworks to keep them agile. Agility in the digital world requires digital technologies that enable data-driven decision-making, swift modifications to business processes, and personalized services. The changes that come with achieving this level of agility have a significant impact on team structures, organizational dynamics, and interactions with external entities. By embracing an Agile culture, companies can navigate the demands of a dynamic marketplace more effectively. They can also embed data-driven decision-making in development processes, leading to improved products and services.

ENVISIONING AN AGILE ORGANIZATION

"What exactly is an agile business and how does the digital world enable it to happen?" In short, it is an organization that anticipates, detects, and responds efficiently and effectively to external and internal change.[4] The characteristics of an Agile organization are not set in stone and can vary depending on the type of business, organizational size, and industry. For example, the banking industry will center around business processes and flexibility driven by data analytics and associated predictions and prescriptions. In contrast, a product-based organization like an auto manufacturer will prioritize inventory and supply chain processes. They may use Robotic Process Automation (RPA) to achieve flexibility and customizability for their product. Finally, a bureaucratic government organization will need to avoid method friction, and a technology-based organization will require an Agile enterprise architecture to accommodate changes in business policies that may arise from analytics.

An Agile organization, as illustrated in Figure 8.1, is one that does the following:

3 Unhelkar, B., 2013, *The Art of Agile Practice: A Composite Approach for Projects and Organizations*, CRC Press (Taylor and Francis Group/an Auerbach Book), Boca Raton, FL, USA.

4 Unhelkar, B., 2018, *Big Data Strategies for Agile Business*, CRC Press (Taylor and Francis Group/an Auerbach Book), Boca Raton, FL, USA.

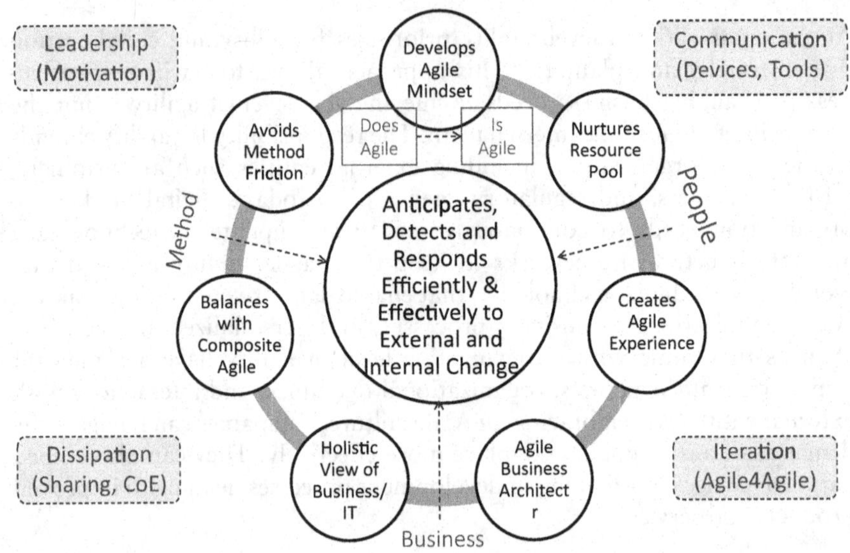

Figure 8.1 Envisioning an Agile Organization and Its Traits for Transformation.

- Develops an Agile mindset across all organizational layers, including teams, departments, divisions, and other organizations. This mindset is a psychological shift from "doing" agile to "being" agile.
- Nurtures a resource pool of Agile capabilities closely supported by digital technology. These capabilities will span technologies, methodologies, and sociological dimensions of the business. Data collection, storage, analytics, and the generation of insights to be used by business processes are part of this resource pool.
- Creates an Agile experience for all stakeholders – technology, business, clients, and customers. The organization can iteratively build on this experience by identifying success stories as use cases across all stakeholders. Communicating the value of agility is important for fostering this agile experience.
- Implements an enterprise business architecture that consolidates current capabilities and makes provisions for future capabilities – especially digital capabilities, including data, tools, and cybersecurity – that are aligned with business goals.
- Maintains a holistic business view across all divisions, departments, and functions of the organization. A holistic view of the business by its leaders ensures that the business is not considered merely a sum of its parts, but rather an organic entity with its personality and gestalt. Only such a holistic view of the business will enable it to be agile and remain agile.

- Applies Composite Agile Methods and Strategies (CAMS) to ensure the proper balance between the agile methodology and the demands from the planned methods in terms of documentation, tools, and contracts.
- Avoids method friction[5] between the myriad standards, frameworks, and approaches in the organization. Development, quality, operations, cybersecurity, compliance, and various other business functions can follow their own method. For example, development can follow Scrum, and quality can follow Six Sigma. Such methods across an organization can result in method friction, which must be avoided in an agile organization.

Achieving true organizational agility goes beyond individuals, teams, and agile practices. "Being agile" is a more abstract concept requires implementation of digital technologies across all levels of an organization. While "being agile" is challenging and complex, it is what ultimately delivers the most value. It involves strategically using data analysis tools that promote a data-driven decision-making culture across the organization. With access to these decision-making tools, each employee can work toward making the organization more agile. To achieve true agility, a harmonious blend of methodology, personnel, and business practices is required amongst all stakeholders.

The following are the support characteristics of Agile organizations, as depicted in Figure 8.1:

- Leadership is crucial in motivating and sustaining Agile change.
- Effective communication across various mediums and with suitable frequencies is another cornerstone of an Agile organization.
- Agile mindset is iterative and incremental, even in Agile adoption.
- Knowledge and experience sharing and diffusion are emphasized in Agile organizations.

Ongoing change management

Transitioning to an Agile organization requires a well-planned change management strategy to ensure a seamless transition and reduce risks.[6] This change management strategy is an ongoing, iterative, and incremental change. Effective technical, process, and social change will depend on proper communication. It is crucial to communicate the benefits of Agility,

5 Unhelkar, B., *Avoiding Method Friction: A CAMS-based Perspective*, Cutter Executive Report, 20 Aug 2012, Vol. 13, No, 6, Agile Product and Project Management Practice, Boston, USA.

6 Creasey, T., 2023, *Adapting and Adjusting Change Management in an Agile Project*, *Prosci*. Available at: www.prosci.com/blog/adapting-and-adjusting-change-management-in-agile (Accessed: 15 July 2023).

as well as its challenges, to all stakeholders in a timely and regular manner. Transitioning to an agile organization will change business processes, and the change-management strategy must include training employees on the new processes and providing comprehensive guidance to help them fully understand the Agile work methods, data, and tools. Involving employees in the process enables addressing their concerns related to change. Becoming Agile results in increased efficiency and improved product and service quality as the outputs relate to the customers' needs and align with the desired business outcomes.

At the individual level, an agile work environment is about owning one's work. This shift in work ethics is supported by heightened visibility of progress on tasks, with the team providing support and the coach acting as a protective barrier. This approach reduces the time and effort required to manage a project or carry out business as usual (BAU), freeing up resources throughout the organization in a subtle yet significant way.[7]

Non-verbal, face-to-face communications

Agile transformations involve significant shifts in organizational communication styles. Collaborative groups become more prevalent, reducing the need for formal and documentation-centric communication. As a result, group dynamics become increasingly crucial. Face-to-face communication with its non-verbal cues becomes an integral part of the workplace. Group structures also impact communication, which in turn, affects group dynamics. Flat organizational structures can simplify communication while daily stand-ups and visible charting make communication ongoing and rapid. The emphasis remains on the non-verbal aspect of communication within and outside the organization. However, digital channels of communication pose challenges with non-verbal communication. To address this, the use of pictures, emojis, and audios where relevant can enrich communication beyond words.

Synthesis and gestalt

In an agile organization, synthesis plays a critical role as it provides a complete and holistic view of the organization and its processes. In today's data-driven world, the organization's various aspects are interconnected, and data from diverse sources is interwoven. Although analysis is a widely accepted problem-solving method, only synthesis can deploy a solution in an agile organization due to the complex interconnectedness of the data. Besides, synthesis offers a snapshot of the organization's behavior, which is crucial

7 Unhelkar, B., *Lean-Agile Tautology*, Cutter Executive Update, April 2014, 3 of 5, Vol. 15, No. 5, Agile Product & Project Management Practice, Boston, MA, USA.

for achieving genuine agility. To be agile, it is not enough to follow agile processes; the psychological concept of gestalt mentioned earlier is equally important. Gestalt prioritizes a comprehensive and interconnected approach to tasks and activities and fosters a synergistic work environment with minimal friction. Overall, gestalt aligns closely with Agile as it prioritizes a comprehensive, interconnected approach over analytical techniques. By being conscious of the collective vibe and gestalt of the workplace, a digital organization moves toward authentic, customer-centric agility.

Effortlessness and unhurriedness

Unhurriedness is an important value in agile work, as highlighted in Chapter 2. Psychologically, unhurriedness means working at a comfortable and sustainable pace without feeling pressured. In this approach, the work process is as important as the output. Effortlessness is a natural outcome of unhurriedness, which can be achieved through sustainable work ethics such as self-ownership, self-direction, and ease of collaboration. Agile organizations also use digital technologies to simplify mundane tasks, thus freeing up time for more creative work. By focusing on creative tasks, organizations become Lean and agile, encapsulating the idea of effortlessness and unhurriedness.

Sustainability in development is less about carbon emissions and more about prioritizing solutions that developers can create without feeling stressed by competition and deadlines. The emphasis is on simplicity and ease. Work is typically associated with effort and lack of joy. Successful agile organizations make work is effortless and joyful because of the noncompetitive and collaborative mindset. Only effortlessness is sustainable. However, effortlessness is not laziness. An effortless work environment is full of positive vibes and enthusiasm, and results in high productivity.

Be-Happen rather than Plan-Do

One interesting psychological observation during Agile transformation exercises is that significant work happens naturally. This gives rise to the idea of "Be-Happen" in agile work. Unlike the "Plan-Do" approach and the "envision-evolve" model of contemporary Agile at the project level, "Be-Happen" is a distinctly different. While it is crucial at an individual level, "Be-Happen" is even more complex but rewarding at the organizational level. Being Agile produces remarkable and favorable outcomes, such as a less task-driven culture, more innovation and communication, and highly supportive. Since being Agile produces much work spontaneously rather than through planned tasks, directing and coordinating the work is challenging. While it may seem risky in an Agile approach that tasks are not planned, measured, and budgeted in the traditional project management sense, these risks are positive because being Agile yields creative outputs. Leaders need courage and psychosocial astuteness to align the work outputs and make "Be-Happen" feasible. This psychosocial astuteness includes sophistication in the use of Transaction Analysis, Maslow's needs hierarchy, MBTI, and other tools discussed.

Multilayered and holistic

Agile is a multi-layered especially at the organizational level. It begins with an individual changing their mindset, followed by forming a cross-functional, co-located team with a small number of cohesive members. Larger groups and divisions are eventually involved, culminating in the entire organization embracing Agile values rather than just the specific ceremonies of Agile. While certain Agile practices, such as Kanban and showcasing, may be limited to a Scrum team, the organization embraces Agile values across all its functions. The multilayered nature of Agile is also evident during an Agile transformation, where Agile concepts are applied to the transformation process. This use of Agile for Agile is possible because Agile is innate to human psychology, and all individuals have a certain amount of ingrained agility. This starting point of agility is used to bootstrap the transformation of an entire organization. Once the bootstrap has kicked in, activities in the organization become more and more holistic. Agile as a work culture approaches any problem comprehensively and is better suited to fulfilling the higher levels of Maslow's hierarchy of needs. Leaders responsible for transformation can satisfy basic levels of the needs hierarchy quickly. As a result, there is greater freedom for employees to practice a holistic approach to problems and solutions.

Delivery and deliverer

The Agile Manifesto gives more importance to individuals and their interactions than simply setting delivery targets and planning tasks accordingly. Therefore, the focus is more on the deliverer rather than the deliverable, and that focus can be applied to a variety of organizational functions beyond just project-based work when an organization transforms into an agile one. The relationship between delivery and deliverer is a crucial psychological factor. Agile methodology emphasizes the creation of visible output that adds value to the user, which is achieved through practices such as sprints, iterations, and daily Scrums that prioritize delivery. However, the sustainability of this focus at an organizational level is a valid concern that must be addressed. While delivery is typically limited to project work, many BAU activities lack incremental deliverables evident in Agile projects. This raises the question of whether Agile can be applied to such areas. Fortunately, it is possible to leverage Agile principles in these cases by shifting the focus from what is delivered to who is delivering it. In this way, Agile can benefit the deliverer as much as the delivery itself, making it an essential tool for any organization looking to optimize its workflow.

Belongingness

One of the most crucial aspects of organizational structure in an Agile setup is the almost tangible sense of belongingness, as described by Maslow's hierarchy of needs. This human need for belongingness is effectively met by an Agile organization through the focus on ownership, self-motivation, and self-organization. By collaborating, Agile team members can contribute directly to the organization's goals without resorting to harmful or unethical behavior, resulting in greater fulfillment, job satisfaction, productivity, and quality. Belongingness is the foundation for the higher levels of Maslow's hierarchy and a non-measurable right-brained attribute. This inability to measure belongingness is a potential reason why it is not sufficiently discussed and implemented in agile transformations. However, business leaders implementing Agile transformation should be aware of this situation and create opportunities for valuable experiences of belongingness. Belongingness and many such factors that are soft and fuzzy, difficult to measure, and yet integral to a successful transition to agile at the organizational level.

ADVANTAGES OF ORGANIZATIONAL AGILE

As an organization adopts an agile approach, its leadership capabilities expand beyond the original precepts of the Agile Manifesto. Despite the challenges that come with its adaptability, Agile remains a highly appealing business leadership approach in the organizational realm. It's not limited to software development but can benefit the broader business space. This is because the business itself gains the most from Agile's implementation. Business agility can be measured by an organization's ability to adapt to changes in its operating environment timely and effective. Agile culture is fascinating as majority stakeholders start to take an active role in prioritization and decision-making. Figure 8.2 shows the increasing levels of awareness from individuals to society that utilize digital capabilities, digital tools, agile training, and experience to help and mentor the entire organization transition to agile. As shown in Figure 8.2, this awareness grows from the individual to the team, the organization, and society. The skill set develops from basic (entry level skills of digital and agile) to expert (able to practice herself the skills of digital and agile) to coach (helping others through coaching and mentoring). While it can be challenging for many business stakeholders to balance the agile tasks with their core business responsibility, their commitment to Agile contributes significantly to the

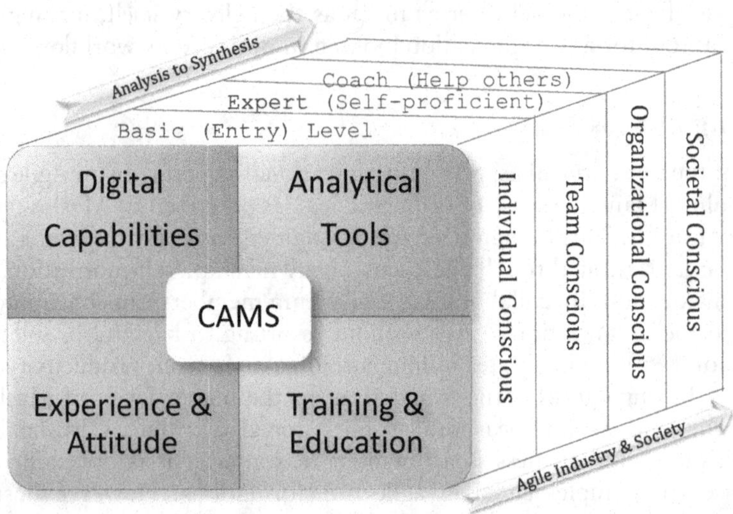

Figure 8.2 Tiers of Awareness and Their Mapping to Agile Working Style.

transition. Agile brings together those who develop solutions and those who will ultimately synergistically use them. This section outlines some key advantages Agile can bring at the organizational level.

Stakeholder collaboration

Agility at the organizational level has numerous advantages, including its ability to bring stakeholders together. The Agile culture fosters collaboration and communication between business and technical stakeholders, creating a clear alignment of work artifacts toward a common goal. In Agile environments, stakeholders are involved throughout the entire project lifecycle, allowing for feedback and necessary adjustments to be made in real time. Customers and end users are also active participants in all aspects of the business, contributing significantly to the creation of new products and services and improving operational processes. This contrasts with organizations that rely on formal, planned approaches, where customers or end users see the final product in the last stage, after testing. The Agile approach removes barriers between consumers and developers, leading to more relevant and higher-quality solutions. Collaborative work throughout the development process reduces the likelihood of rework, resulting in a project outcome of direct value to the business. While delivering work on time and within budget is important, it is not the main goal of stakeholder collaboration. Communication is critical in this process; regular check-ins and updates keep everyone informed and engaged. Successful stakeholder collaboration leads to a project outcome that meets the needs of all involved parties.

Fail-fast across the board

The "Fail-fast" principle, also discussed in the previous chapter, is a crucial aspect of Agile approach, particularly at the organizational level. It involves addressing the evolving layers of Maslow's hierarchy of needs to create a secure and comfortable environment where individuals are better equipped to accept failures as non-judgmental events. "Fail-fast" creates exciting opportunities for experimentation and taking positive risks. Agile's iterative and incremental nature further supports the acceptance of failures by allowing for rapid testing and iterations before major issues arise. Ongoing conversations among stakeholders can identify opportunities and risks from both business and technical perspectives while detecting errors in technologies, architectures, and processes. "Fail fast, fail often" is a common mantra in both Lean and Agile, and the iterative nature of Agile supports this mindset. The overall output quality is significantly improved by continuously learning from failures and making necessary adjustments.

Paradox absorption

Agile methodology can seem paradoxical in many ways. Despite being associated with a more creative, right-brained approach, Agile inherently involves risk and uncertainty. The entire Agile Manifesto is at risk of being misread as anti-planning, which it is not. Many aspects of Agile are not clearly definable or measurable. Agile is, thus, paradoxical. For example, Agile helps with rapid development, but the delivery can be clogged without sufficient tools. Agile can free team members from the burden of task-driven management but lays additional responsibilities for collaboration. Agile is sustainable but the leader has to coordinate the outputs. Agile's iterative delivery is a change of mindset but allows organizations to quickly identify and address potential issues.

Ultimately, Agile's adaptable, right-brained approach allows it to handle contradictions and complexity effectively compared with planned methods dominated by left-brain thinking, which are often linear, with predetermined and quantifiable outcomes. The left brain prefers well-defined organizational structures and becomes agitated when things are fuzzy. Paradoxes can be particularly challenging for left-brain thinking, whereas right-brained agility embraces the ability to navigate ambiguity and complexity.

As individuals, groups, and organizations progress toward the higher levels of Maslow's hierarchy, they embrace another important Agile core value: courage. Originally, courage in Agile referred to the ability to abandon flawed solution designs or code and start anew. However, courage also involves relinquishing the comfort and false sense of security accompanying rigid hierarchy and planning in favor of a more flexible and adaptable approach. For business leaders, transitioning from a formal and planned working style dominated by left-brain thinking to a more Agile, facilitative approach driven by right-brain thinking also requires courage. Courage is the ultimate capability of a brain to absorb paradoxes.

Industrial leanness

The interdependence of businesses in the digital world creates a positive situation. When one business organization transforms into an agile work culture, all other associated businesses are also nudged toward becoming agile. This is because when one digital business process becomes agile, all other processes with which it collaborates must also become agile. An Agile environment promotes frequent communication with business partners and regulatory entities, positively impacting the industry. An Agile organization can influence the working style of other entities it comes into contact with, extending its reach beyond immediate responsibilities.

Agile is also Lean because it eliminates all unnecessary activities.[8] This leanness of business processes impacts multiple, collaborating organizations across industries. By emphasizing eliminating waste and optimizing value, the Lean processes allow teams to streamline how solutions are developed and deployed, resulting in overall efficiency for all collaborating businesses. Lean processes enable teams to prioritize tasks and ensure they provide value to end users throughout the development cycle. This prioritization is similar to that in agile. Agile can optimize resource allocation, procurement, and inventory management by providing visibility into internal processes and continuously testing and simplifying them. As a result, businesses can improve the quality and efficiency of their processes. Given its focus on optimization, Lean and agile complement each other to render an industry agile.

Joy of working

It's important to consider how agile culture at an organizational level can improve the quality of work life. There was no place for joy in earlier approaches to work, such as PMBOK and PRINCE2. Work was seen as a burden, and enjoying it was an alien concept. However, agile culture has changed this perception and created a workplace full of humor, fun, and relaxation. This does not mean that the workplace becomes an

8 Unhelkar, B., *Lean-Agile Tautology*, Cutter Executive Update, April 2014, 3 of 5, Vol. 15, No. 5, Agile Product & Project Management Practice, Boston, MA, USA.

entertainment venue. Agile culture is non-competitive and unhurried and promotes extensive communication and cooperation among team members. As a result, the political maneuvering and territorialism in a workplace are kept to a minimum. Understanding right-brain functioning and its application in agile methodology can be incredibly valuable in reducing the stress of competition. Agile culture values trust, collaboration, and support, encouraging a natural flow of creativity. Work is free to progress without undue pressure within this collaborative space. In agile work environments, people work together toward a common goal and don't worry about who gets the credit. This non-competitive spirit also means failure is accepted, and work becomes a source of joy. Therefore, potential setbacks are identified and addressed more quickly through the team's collective efforts.

A global agricultural bank transitioning to Agile shared an interesting visual aid on their Kanban wall. The picture depicted a chariot with four horses, each labeled as "Product Owners," "Business Analysts," "Developers," or "Testers." The "Architects" and "Senior Management" were assigned to the wheels while the "Agile Coach" was the charioteer. The team enthusiastically embraced this clever visualization, and their leadership supported it, showcasing the childlike spirit that often flourishes in successful Agile environments.

Kaizen represents non-competitiveness in Agile environments. The term is composed of "Kai," meaning change, and "Zen," which is often translated as "good," and it represents small, continuous improvements. Interestingly, the origin of "Zen" in Kaizen can be traced back to the Sanskrit word "Dhyâna," which refers to meditation. Adopting a meditative mindset in daily work significantly benefits an Agile organizational culture. The ability to remain centered while facilitating ongoing, incremental change is a cornerstone of Agile practice, much like meditation in psychological disciplines. Agile's paradoxical nature reflects Zen's essence, emphasizing individual interactions, accepting failures and "being" more than "doing" Agile. The success of Agile depends on embracing and navigating these paradoxes with skill and insight.

CONSOLIDATION WORKSHOP

1. What is your opinion on the most intriguing agile trait from a psychosocial perspective at an organizational level? Can you provide a detailed example to support your answer?
2. Why should agile spread across the organization and the industry as a whole? Why should it not be limited to the development work for which it was originally designed? Please provide a comprehensive explanation backed by examples.

3. How would you differentiate effortlessness from laziness in your own words? Can you provide an in-depth analysis, with examples and scholarly sources to support your answer?
4. What is the difference between analysis and synthesis? How important is synthesis in agile work at the organizational level?
5. Can things "happen" without "doing" them? Discuss in the context of the psychology of agile.
6. Please explain how Agile is considered a holistic approach. Can you provide a detailed response, including examples and scholarly sources?
7. Why is paradoxical thinking considered an essential characteristic of agile?
8. From the perspective of Kaizen, why is "non-competitiveness" an integral part of Agile? Can you provide a detailed response supported by scholarly sources?
9. Is belongingness important at the organizational level? Discuss based on Maslow's needs hierarchy and agile.

Index

Printed in the United States
by Baker & Taylor Publisher Services

Printed in the United States
by Baker & Taylor Publisher Services